# Beaded Jewelry

## ⚫-➤ The Complete Guide ◆-⚫

Susan Ray

©2007 Susan Ray
Published by

 **krause publications**

*An Imprint of F+W Publications*

**700 East State Street • Iola, WI 54990-0001**
**715-445-2214 • 888-457-2873**
**www.krausebooks.com**

Our toll-free number to place an order or obtain a free catalog is (800) 258-0929.

NOTE: These instructions are made available for your entertainment and enjoyment. They are not intended for commercial use.

The following registered trademark terms, products, books, magazines and companies appear in this publication: A Bead Timeline; Bead Style; Beadazzled, Inc.; Beadazzled, Where Beads and Inspiration Meet; Beadwork; Bejeweled™ Software Co.; Bullseye Glass Co.; Cas Webber Photography; Contemporary Lampworking; Copper Loom; Delica®; E6000 Glue; Ebb Designs; Effetre; Fire Mountain Gems and Beads®; Frantz Art Glass & Supply; Galena Beads; Georgia O'Keeffe Museum; Google™; Griffin Silk; G-S Hypo Tube Cement; Hot Stuff Special "T"™ Illusion Glue; Jewelry Arts & Lapidary Journal; Jewelry Designer Manager™ Software; Judikins Inc.; Knot Just Beads; Lauscha; Making Glass Beads; McKenzie Glassworks; Mont Rest; Moretti; MSN®; National Geographic Society; National Public Radio; Nymo Thread; Polarfleece®; Polyform Products Co.; Premo!™ Polymer Clay; Professional Deluxe Coiling Gizmo®; Rio Grande®; Riverstone Bead Co.; Rust-Oleum®; Satake; Satellite City; Sculpey® Clay, Glaze and Texture Sheets; Sculpey® MoldMaker & Polymer Clay Conditioner; Skewer Beads; Skinner Method; Soft Touch™; Soft Flex® Co.; Super Glue; Super Peg; Swarovski; Teflon®; The Bead Museum, Washington, D.C.; The Bead Society of Greater Washington; The Clay Store™; The Coiling Gizmo® and Econo Winder; The Corning Museum; The History of Beads; The International Society of Glass Beadmakers; The School of Beadwork; Third International Bead Conference; Tupperware®; Vintaj Natural Brass Co.™; WigJig® Centaur, Cyclops and Delphi; William L. Allen photos; Yellow Pages™.

Library of Congress Catalog Number: 2006935753
ISBN 13: 978-0-89689-385-6
ISBN 10: 0-89689-385-5
Edited by Shelley Coffman
Designed by Rachael Knier

Printed in China

# DEDICATION
*To Juli Ikonomopoulos*

Over the past five years, Juli has been there to help create *Easy Beaded Jewelry, Organic Beaded Jewelry* and now, *Beaded Jewelry The Complete Guide*. Of course, the talent of many goes into making every book a reality, but without Juli, without her patience, talents and friendship, the hard work involved in these endeavors would have been insurmountable. Juli's unwavering commitment to excellence and her vast skill at editing every word (and her own love of beading jewelry) have made my ramblings understandable and brief. Anyone who knows Juli understands she comes to every project with a smile and works through every task with endless energy, always anticipating every need. Juli, I can never thank you enough for setting what spilled from my heart into such discerning text. Thank you for being a partner in these enormous undertakings and thank you for your dedication and your friendship.

— Susan Ray

*Juli Ikonomopoulos: Kyanite Out on the Town Necklace.*

# IN MEMORIAM
Patricia Karl, whose generous heart filled every room with laughter and love.

*Eileen Feldman: My Heart's Delight Necklace.*

# ACKNOWLEDGMENTS

I would like to thank the following people for their individual contributions in bringing this book to life:

- Joyce Diamanti, whose thoughtful foreword helps us vividly relive beading from the beginning of time.

- Penelope Diamanti, for her trust and pouring her heart into the mammoth task of creating a virtual tour of one of her latest retail storefronts, and her willingness to share not only the talents of so many top designers that grace these pages, but allowing us to get a bird's-eye view of her life as one of the finest bead champions in the world today.

- Cas Webber, for her design talent, enthusiasm and gracious photographic skills, including close-ups and how-tos for the talented designers from Beadazzled.

*Cindy Yost and Kat Allison: Copper Loop Amber Bracelet.*

- Sue Wilke, for her friendship and allowing me to re-create her personal style for us all.

- Candy Wiza, Krause Publications project editor for *Organic Beaded Jewelry* and now my acquisition editor, for her intellectual sparring, creativity, love and laughter.

- Susan Sliwicki, Krause Publications editor, for her discerning eye and clarity.

- Brenda Mazemke, for her lasting support and encouragement.

- Rachael Knier, Krause Publications graphic designer, for her creativity to set every page with such an artful eye.

- Kris Kandler, for the Krause Publications studio photography gracing so many of these pages insightfully.

- William L. Allen, for the genius in his photographs of the dazzling Beadazzled store in Tyson, Va., and his kind generosity.

- James Lankton, for the generous reprints from his book *A Bead Timeline, Volume I, Prehistory to 1200 CE,* with credits to Robert Liu and Joyce Diamanti in service.

- LeRoy Goertz, once again, for his dedication to perfection and for providing us informative and skilled techniques with the Coiling Gizmo.

- Gary Helwig, for his encouragement, support and sharing, and for giving us your time, talent and skills both on and off of the WigJig.

- Barbara Carleton of the Bejeweled Software Co., for sharing her own jewelry skills with such generosity and style.

- Trish Italia, Jan Ketza Harris and Jessica Italia of Galena Beads, for sharing their special designer musings.

- The talented lampwork artists, who again gave so generously of their work: Karen and Bob Leonardo and Michelle McKenzie.

- Lynn Larkins, for once again amazing us with her skill using metal clay.

- Polymer artists Sheila Hobson and Tracy Callahan, who continue to share magical designs made with this wondrous medium.

- Kat Allison and Cindy Yost, for sharing their creative talents for making bead landscapes on their resourceful loom.

- Wendy Mullane and Jeanne Holland of Vintaj Natural Brass Co., for their laughter, enthusiasm, support, and, most importantly, sharing their love of vintage findings and reviving their use almost single-handedly.

- The many wonderfully talented jewelry designers: Barbara Carleton, Sherrie Chapin, Darien Kaiser, Eileen Feldman, Jan Ketza Harris, Jeanne Holland, Jessica Italia, Trish Italia, Susan A. Karczewski, Deanna and Janet Killackey, Sue Kwong and Karen Li, Dotsie S. Mack, Kathleen Manning, Barbara Markoe, Deborah McClintock, Jenni Moore, Mackenzie Mullane, Wendy Mullane, Christy Nicholas, Monique Roberson, Cathie Roberts, Megan Starkey, Ronda Terry, Jessica Tracey, Cas K. Webber, Sandi Webster, Sue Wilke and Ilene Baranowitz.

*Jeanne Holland: Olive Jade Passion.*

- Once again, to Tracy Callahan, for being my rock when I needed her most.

- Chris Baker, for sharing her beautiful B&B, Mont Rest, tranquility, love and friendship.

- Kevin, for his ability to make me smile and his ever-patient understanding, and always his love.

- Eric and Velvette, for lighting my life with so much hope for tomorrow.

# TABLE OF CONTENTS

## Chapter Six: Stringing Basics (continued)

*Sandi Webster: Desert Sands Necklace and Bracelet.*

*Beads of Antiquity. Courtesy of Beadazzled. Photography by William L. Allen.*

# INTRODUCTION

Historically, beads have been thought to chase ill will, heal the sick, cure broken hearts, and serve as a partner in prayer, a master at magic spells, adornment for kings and babes, a method of legal tender and a broker of accords. From the four corners of the world and within every civilization since the beginning of time, beads have played a role in our outstretched reach forward. They are responsible for raising social status and divine inspiration.

What is the attraction? Where does it come from? Beads seem to reflect the needs of all human beings. Their qualities have become a mirror to our desires and comfort to our souls. Our fascination with them seems to be almost intrinsic. Most importantly, they have helped us to forge community among individuals and commerce among societies. From what we make of these tiny recorders of humanity, here and abroad, our hearts seem to travel with them.

From novice crafters to advanced bead enthusiasts, a lasting and planned community of beading arises. From the importer to the shopkeeper, from the writer, to you at home, possibly taking your first step into the world of jewelry design, we share a passion for beads and a connection to each other. Beads open the world wide and from the portal of our homes and our workplaces, the world also becomes a smaller place.

Buying, selling and trading beads and making jewelry are loves that we share. Within these pages is the best of this community, generously given by some talented and very dedicated jewelry designers and those behind the scenes who have made this book a reality. It is their love and generosity that is yours for the asking.

Beading, whether craft or fine art, hinges us together as friends, enthusiasts and markers of a place in time. We have a responsibility to carry the past forward and reach into the barrel of contemporary bead work to find the glue that joins us together.

Special wishes on your journey.

— Susan Ray

*All jewelry is measured without clasps. All earrings are measured dangles only, without ear wire. If you use a different clasp or ear wire, your finished size will change. To increase length, add more beads. To decrease length, remove a few beads. Always measure twice and crimp once.*

*Courtesy of Beadazzled.*
*Photography by Cas Webber.*

# FOREWORD

*By Joyce Diamanti*

Beads have been with us since the dawn of humanity. Among the earliest, most universal and most enduring artifacts made by man, beads have been used by every culture on earth, from prehistory to the present, and worn by men and women, rich and poor, old and young. Today, beads continue to proliferate in a wildly popular worldwide phenomenon that transcends space and time and has captivated three generations of our family — from my late mother, an early bead enthusiast who inspired all of us, to my daughter Penelope (see more information about Penelope Diamanti, pages 208-210), a dedicated "bead wallah" who has made beads her life's work.

What I love most about beads is learning about them and sharing what I have learned with others, mainly through writing and presenting "Bead Appreciation," an educational program my husband and I developed for schools and museums in which we display and talk about ancient, ethnic and contemporary beads from our collection. In 1995, I chaired the Third International Bead Conference to raise seed money to found The Bead Museum of the Bead Society of Greater Washington. In an awestruck report on that event for National Public Radio, a "beadazzled" Susan Stamberg exclaimed, "Gee, if beads could talk!" Well, they can. Beads are born communicators, and what tales they have to tell! Beads speak to us not only about the impulse to adorn, but about human technical and artistic ingenuity, about social organization and trading patterns, about people's hopes and fears, faith and beliefs.

*Courtesy of Ashes to Beauty Adornments.*

*Many paleoanthropologists, who study early man, believe that beads can tell us much about what makes us human. By four million years ago, our ancestors were walking on two legs, freeing their hands for other tasks. By two million years ago, **Homo habilis,** or "handy man," was crafting crude stone tools that changed little over thousands of generations. About 130,000 years ago, anatomically modern humans appeared, but only toward the end of the Old Stone Age, or Paleolithic period, did **Homo sapiens,** or "intelligent man," show a capacity for abstract thinking, which is the basis of language, both spoken and written, and fundamental to all art and science.*

*Beads are among the earliest evidence of this cultural advance. Of no utilitarian value, beads were used, scientists believe, as abstract symbols. Beads also express other traits that distinguish us as human, including artistic creativity and technological inventiveness. As examples of artistry, they are more than twice as old as Europe's cave paintings. In terms of technology, beads are three times older than the earliest evidence of pottery and textiles.*

With a little study, beads can answer most of your frequently asked questions, such as: Where were they made? When? How? What are they made of? But far more fascinating is what beads can tell us about people. Today, research about the human affinity for beads over tens of thousands of years is uncovering new information about beadmakers and is pursuing answers to related questions, such as:

- Who supplied beadmakers with materials?

- How were their tools and techniques developed?

- What inspired their designs?

- Who traded beads, and what routes did they take?

- Who assembled beads and strung them?

- Who wore beads, and how did they wear them?

- How else have people used beads?

- Why have people treasured beads over the millennia?

*See page 162 for more about the Monk Special design by Monique Roberson.*

*Courtesy of Beadazzled.*
*Photography by Cas Webber.*

The first objects used as beads were probably flowers, seeds and similar materials that have not survived. The oldest known extant beads are tiny shells that were painstakingly perforated in southern Africa 75,000 years ago. While undeniably decorative and technically innovative, early beads are thought to have originated, not as the result of some artistic inspiration or love of tinkering, but primarily as a symbolic means of communication. After tools, to take care of basic needs for food, shelter and possibly clothing, beads were the first type of artifacts to be widely produced. By 40,000 years ago, beads were being made in quantity in a variety of new materials not only in Africa, but in Europe, Asia and Australia. What sort of information did these early beadmakers so urgently need to communicate?

The proliferation of beads in the late Paleolithic period might have been triggered by the need to meet the challenges of population growth and environmental change as *Homo sapiens* spread out of Africa and across the globe. In order to flourish, beads, like language, needed company — a community eager to share information. Beads with socially shared meanings could convey vital information in a world of increasingly complex communities.

Within groups, these abstract symbols could facilitate everyday life by identifying individuals in terms of age, sex, marital status and fertility; prowess as a provider or warrior; wealth; and/or social rank. Among groups, beads and other ornaments could help distinguish friend from foe, express broader relationships of rank and power, further the exchange of goods and ideas, and reinforce ties within a larger ethnic community. Over the millennia, the symbolism of personal adornment would become correspondingly more complex as nomadic bands settled in villages, cities and states arose, and empires spanned the known world.

*People have used beads not only to communicate with one another but to cope with unseen forces of nature. Throughout history, people have attributed all sorts of marvelous properties to ornaments of certain shapes, colors or materials. Early beads and pendants made of animal bone, teeth and tusks probably were worn as talismans that could bring success to the hunter and victory to the warrior. Amuletic female figurines with swelling bellies and beads shaped like pendant breasts may have assured expectant mothers safe delivery of healthy offspring.*

*Burials containing beads suggest that early peoples also looked to these symbols to appeal to supernatural forces for protection and assistance in the afterlife. When formal religion developed, beads and pendants continued to figure prominently in funerary ritual, especially in ancient Egypt, where a pendant in the form of a sacred scarab ensured the deceased passage to paradise.*

*Courtesy of Beadazzled.*
*Photography by William L. Allen.*

Today, beads still have spiritual uses, most notably in Hindu, Buddhist, Muslim and Catholic prayer strands. While amulets reflect the concerns of people who lived in different times and circumstances, they also echo certain enduring and universal feelings — the desire for success and abundance, the longing for love and children, the fear of death and hope for immortality, the belief that good can triumph over evil.

The way early beads and pendants were worn — strung on a thong and prominently displayed — no doubt enhanced their effectiveness as communicators, with constant contact with the body to increase their amuletic power. And then, as now, beads also would have enhanced a person's

*Evening Passion Necklace.*
*Courtesy of Jan Ketza Harris.*

appearance and increased one's attractiveness. Reaching out to the viewer, beads command, "Look at me!" While intimately embracing the wearer, beads whisper, "Come hither!" These aspects of beads have tended to fuse over time, and today, beads have become primarily, but not solely, objects of adornment. They are still imbued with amuletic magic and are a wonderful way to express one's individuality.

Beads are also bound up with the more material side of cultural evolution. As Paleolithic peoples explored new environments, beadmakers developed

new tools to exploit new materials. The oldest known metal artifacts are copper beads. Later, beads would be among the earliest examples of glass.

The development of sophisticated stoneworking and metalworking techniques increased efficiency and led to a profusion of new bead shapes and designs. As society became more stratified, a growing demand by the emerging elite for beads and ornaments was met by new patterns of supply and production. Innovations included mining and systematic collection of bead materials; intensive bead manufacture in serial stages, representing an investment of thousands of hours of group activity, with craft specialization and division of labor; and organized transport and trade of bead materials and finished beads, which would evolve from face-to-face barter into vast trade networks stretching to the farthest regions of the world.

The bead trade is almost as old as beads themselves. While many bead materials are found locally, highly prized materials often come from distant sources. Ancient beads made

*Courtesy of Beadazzled.*
*Photography by Cas Webber.*

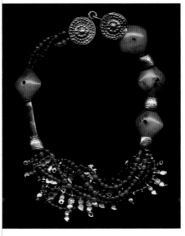

*Courtesy of Ashes to Beauty Adornments.*

of seashells have been found high in the Himalayas and the Andes, deep in the African rain forest, and in the arid desert of the American Southwest — hundreds of miles from the ocean. Prehistoric trade in coral was followed by trade in amber, lapis lazuli and hard stones such as carnelian, rock crystal and agate.

By the Bronze Age, long-distance trade in these precious materials extended to Scandinavia, Japan, Indonesia and sub-Saharan Africa. Beginning around 400 B.C., beads and bead materials traveled maritime routes through the Mediterranean and the Red Sea to the Indian Ocean and beyond, to Africa, Southeast Asia and Korea. Overland they followed the Silk Road, which linked Imperial Rome to India and China. With the rise of Islam, Arab trade networks carried beads south across the Sahara and north into Scandinavia via the Vikings. When Columbus landed in the Bahamas in 1492, he offered the islanders strings of beads — the first symbolic communication between the Old World and the New. In the Age of

Exploration, thousands of tons of beads from Venice, and later, Bohemia, were traded to Africa, Asia and the Americas.

From the beginning, the exchange of ideas and technology has accompanied this lively long-distance bead trade. Today, the volume of trade continues to grow, and its pace accelerates ever more rapidly. This interchange takes place on a worldwide scale, and producers rarely meet consumers. You might ask, "If beads can talk, can they also walk?" Well, they don't have feet, but they do have traders to connect this far-flung bead community. A web of buyers and sellers on many levels — collectors/distributors, exporters/importers, wholesalers/retailers — support the makers and supply the users, bringing us beads from the ends of the earth. And the symbiotic bond that binds us all together is our common love of beads, creating unity in diversity as culturally different groups share bead styles and traditions and make exotic beads their own. Multiculturalism is flowering in our global village.

## A BEAD TIMELINE
VOLUME I: PREHISTORY to 1200CE

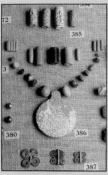

JAMES W. LANKTON

*Courtesy of James W. Lankton, M.D.*
*See The Bead Museum in our*
*Resource Guide, page 214, for copies.*

**A BEAD TIMELINE, VOLUME I: PREHISTORY TO 1200.**

*A Bead Timeline at The Bead Museum in Washington, D.C., brings together more than
5,000 beads in a visual panorama that helps the viewer follow the story of beads
through space and time. In this U-shaped display, beads are arranged in geographic
bands and in chronological sequence from prehistory to the present, over 38 linear feet.
The oldest beads date to about 12,000 years ago; the newest are 21st century creations.
The timeline is a work in progress, with additions at either end and points in between as
new beads are acquired and we learn more about them.*

*A companion catalog,* **A Bead Timeline, Volume I: Prehistory to 1200** *complements the
earlier part of this permanent exhibit. Photographs by Robert K. Liu of some 2,300 beads
and text by James W. Lankton, M.D., put the beads in cultural context and relate them to
the people who made, traded and used them, enhancing viewers' understanding of the
exhibit and bringing the Timeline to a wider audience.*

**Bead Timeline, the Catalog,** *and* **The Bead Museum** *are the fruit of the collaborative
efforts of members of the* **Bead Society of Greater Washington** *to fulfill the society's
mission, which is to study beads and share information with others. To learn more about
other exhibits, programs and activities of The Bead Museum and the Bead Society of
Greater Washington, visit the Web site www.beadmuseumdc.org or www.bsgw.org.*

# CHAPTER ONE

# THE LOOK THAT'S RIGHT FOR YOU

# PERSONAL STYLE
*With Sue Wilke*

*Sue Wilke: Signature from Easy Beaded Jewlery.*

*Courtesy of Beadazzled.*
*Photography by William L. Allen.*

Are you intrigued by the possibilities of designing and making jewelry? Where to start? Your personal style may be professional and polished or classic and elegant. You may be comfortable and casual, or earthy and understated. Do friends describe you as fun and flamboyant or a dedicated romantic? Or do you believe "variety is the spice of life?"

Begin by shopping. Go window shopping, first for ideas, then jewelry styles and beads. When looking for your personal style, you will find inspiration everywhere. Start by looking at ready-made jewelry designs, such as those in this book. Visit your specialty bead store. They will likely have sample pieces for inspiration. Look in magazines, catalogs, fashion boutiques and department stores. What styles do you consistently gravitate toward?

Keep a journal. Clip magazine photos. Sketch out designs. The more ideas you collect that are truly appealing to you, the more clearly you will see your design style developing. Maybe only part of a piece of jewelry gives you an idea, like a certain closure or dangle. Make a note of it. Now you have begun your own personal "idea and style" file.

*Michelle McKenzie: Palladium Bracelet.*
*Courtesy of McKenzie Glassworks.*

Once you begin to discover your personal jewelry style, your design sense will emerge. Do you prefer symmetrical or asymmetrical patterns? What size beads appeal to you? Do you love the natural feel of gemstones? Or the sparkle of crystals? It's not just the physical size — how about your personality? Large, bold jewelry definitely says "look at me" more loudly than a simple, tailored strand of pearls. Inventory your wardrobe and your jewelry box. What type of jewelry do you commonly wear? There are no right or wrong answers. The style a woman displays — through her clothes, purses, shoes and, yes, jewelry — says a lot when she enters a room. Creativity comes in all styles.

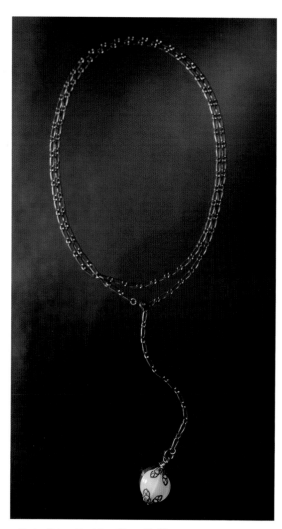

The technique is in the clasp! Wear this long, wear this double-wrapped, wear this triple-wrapped. Add a pendant to the 8mm jump ring and clip it anywhere into the chain for a long Y-connector drop style. Or, double wrap with a Y-connector drop style. Wear it as a belt or with your belt. The sky is the limit. Just clip and go!

— Darien Kaiser

*Darien Kaiser: Capricious Charm Necklace.*

# DOWN TO SIZE

*With Trish Italia*

The definition of petite is small, little, diminutive, tiny.

Petite does not necessarily mean just small or tiny. If you are a petite person and you like larger chunky jewelry, you can still get that look by using beads or pendants that are scaled down to a smaller size.

Start by looking through magazines, books and catalogs and seeing what TV anchors and talk show hosts are wearing. When you find your style, the next step is finding the beads on a smaller scale. Many beads come in a variety of sizes. You might have a choice of small, medium or large beads from the category of your choosing. Pearls come in various sizes, too.

**NOTE:** When searching for beads that will fit with your body type, you might need to go only as far as your jewelry box. Examining beads on necklaces you already wear will give you a hint about what size beads make you feel comfortable. Once you have an idea in mind and beads of the proper size, then it's time to string.

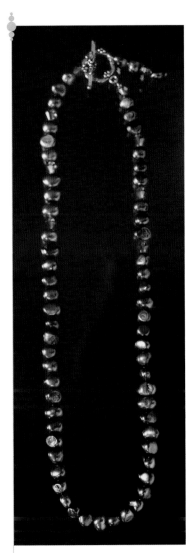

*Trish Italia: Purple Passion Pearl Necklace.*

*Courtesy of Beadazzled. Photography by William L. Allen.*

*Courtesy of Beadazzled. Photography by William L. Allen.*

# COLORS THAT FIT

*With Sue Wilke*

Everyone has a favorite color or colors. When you start shopping for beads, you will naturally gravitate toward your favorites. Color palettes can reveal styles — earth tones, pastels, brights. What jewelry colors do you wear? They will also tend to blend with the colors already in your closet.

Soon you will be shopping for clothes to go with your jewelry. Do you suppose that's how the little black dress got created? What a great background for any designer jewelry!

Michelle McKenzie: Jungle Bracelet.
Courtesy of McKenzie Glassworks.

**COLOR CAN CHANGE THE MOOD OF ANY JEWELRY PIECE**

• Cool tones of purples, blues and blue-greens are soothing, like the ebb and flow of the ocean.

• Warm yellow-greens, yellow, orange and red are intense and passionate.

• Whites, blacks, browns, grays, pearls and transparent clear beads are neutral. They reduce the tension and are very sophisticated.

• Metallics, such as gold, silver, pewter and bronze, add richness and reflect light (as do crystals and the luminosity of pearls).

Jan Ketza Harris: Colorplay I Necklace.
Lampwork by Karen Leonardo.

*Jan Ketza Harris: Painting Phis Necklace.*
*Courtesy of Galena Beads.*

# COLORPLAY

*With Jan Ketza Harris*

As you enter the Georgia O'Keeffe Museum in Santa Fe, N. Mex., you see a statement by the artist on the gallery wall. "I can say more with color than I can with words," it reads.

I found I could say things with color and shapes that I couldn't say any other way — things I had no words for. There are moments in life that you will always remember, however old you are. You remember the weather, the smells, the atmosphere, what color you were wearing. It is kept inside your soul forever.

*Jan Ketza Harris: Object of Desire Red Flame Necklace.
Courtesy of Galena Beads.*

in this manner, you become more playful, and the joy of what you create comes through your art. From the tiniest of anklets to the longest lariat necklace, your designs can be enhanced by this discovery.

Pablo Picasso spent a lifetime remembering what it was like to paint as a child. We all have to stop in our busy lives and think back to when we were children coloring. If you can't, find a child, and watch her color. It is children's reckless abandon I admire. They have the courage to create whatever they want, with whatever color they desire. This is colorplay.

The day I read O'Keeffe's statement, my life as an artist changed. My heart pounded with great joy, for I knew what she was saying. My switch was on and I started to look at everything differently. When I started to create, I began with, "What statement am I going to make with color?" By approaching any type of art

*Courtesy of Galena Beads, Galena, Ill.*

**An exercise in colorplay:** Purchase fat quarters (¼ yard samples of fabrics) that appeal to your playfulness. Lay them out, and just study the colors in each piece of fabric. Study the relationship each color has next to another. Select one.

Go to your bead table and find beads that are the same colors as the swatch. Place them in a pile, and mix them up. Take your finger and clear the center like you are making a circle shape. You should have a circle of beads. Here you have your first vision of what a necklace or bracelet would look like with all the colors you admired from the swatch. Do this exercise with all the swatches and develop your playful skills.

Leave these swatches out in view for several weeks. Let them subconsciously seep into your mind. I call this "living with color," living with your art. Sometimes I carry a project with me and look at it throughout the day. I let my mind study it. When I am ready to complete the design, my mind knows what to do, and colors and patterns flow naturally.

Personally, I feel the best artists are the ones who are self-taught. There is a lot to say about that. Respond to your intuition and create colorful jewelry. Every piece will come out fresh, real and alive. Artists strive to do this with every experience. Permit yourself to be experimental. Thank you, Georgia O'Keeffe.

*When you find a color combination you really enjoy using, make a color chip using the same beads on a 4" headpin. Later, when you are stumped for a creative idea, look through these color chips and before you know it, creativity stirs! Collect your chips on large key rings for handy access.*

*— Sue Wilke*

*Jan Ketza Harris: Colorplay II Bracelet. Lampwork by Karen Leonardo.*

*Karen Leonardo: Pharoh beads/Ancients series.*

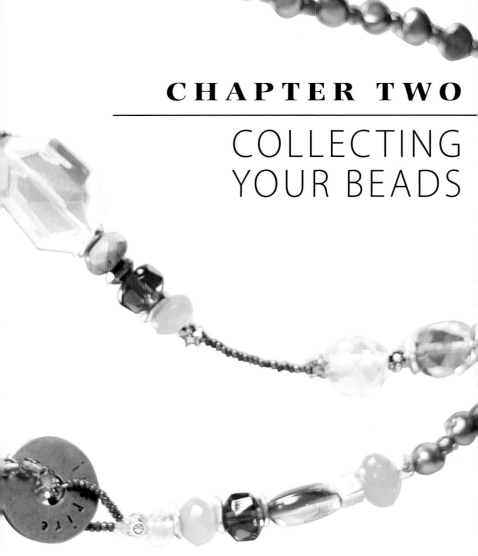

# CHAPTER TWO

## COLLECTING
## YOUR BEADS

# WHERE TO FIND YOUR FAVORITE BEADS

*With Sue Wilke and Susan Ray*

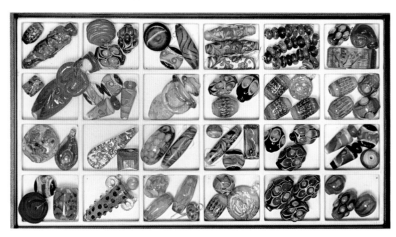

*Courtesy of Beadazzled. Photography by William L. Allen.*

*Courtesy of Beadazzled. Photography by William L. Allen.*

When you become interested in beads, you will find them everywhere. The most obvious place to start looking is at large art supply, craft and sewing stores. They will carry a wide selection, including some craft-quality and some jewelry-quality beads and supplies.

Craft stores are good suppliers for basic beading materials, but if you want something special, go to the specialists. Use the Yellow Pages, local newspapers, bead magazines or Web site searches to find specialty bead shops or those that serve your area. They will be your best source for the widest variety from basic stock to unique beads and findings.

*Michelle McKenzie: Green Frit Series. Lampwork by Michelle McKenzie.*

Specialty bead stores can be intimi-dating to the novice beader, but once you understand the layout of the store, you will be able to find the beads, findings and tools of your choice in no time.

## Specialty Bead Stores

*Courtesy of Beadazzled. Photography by William L. Allen.*

When visiting your local bead store, don't be afraid to talk to the shop owner. Many store owners will happily tell you about the history of the beads you have purchased. It is a treasure to know about the lampwork artist who made the beads, or why the Venetians make their glass on the island of Murano, Italy, or what semiprecious stones were used to enhance a design.

Other specialty shops that feature needlework, fibers and yarns also can be an unexpected source for beads. Art galleries and museum gift shops usually sell unique jewelry. Some sell art glass and lampwork beads by various artists.

*Courtesy of Beadazzled.*
*Photography by William L. Allen.*

*Courtesy of Beadazzled. Photography by William L. Allen.*

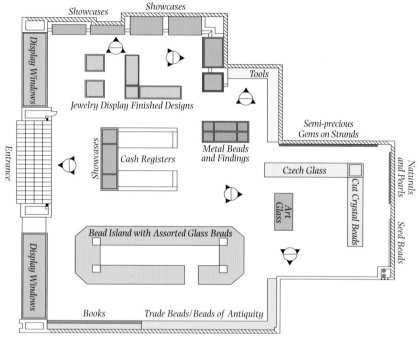

*Map courtesy of Beadazzled. Illustrator: Shawn Stigstell.*

## Anatomy of a Bead Store

At first glance, a store that specializes in beads can seem overwhelming, and although specialty stores are as individual as their owners themselves, all bead stores have many common elements. The map illustrates typical locations for many items available. Acquaint yourself with each area. Your treasure hunting will be more rewarding if it is limited to your search for the right bead and not where to find it within the store.

Search online auctions by typing into the search cue: "glass beads," "hanks of glass beads," "lampwork," "art beads," "seed beads" or "druks." When buying beads in online auctions, consider:

• The seller's feedback score.

• Shipping charges (seller's location).

• Handling charges (applied by seller).

• A bead's actual size—photographs can be deceiving. When in doubt, ask. Reputable sellers will be happy to answer all of your questions. (See our Bead Size Chart, page 71, for assistance.)

Also note that buying more than one item from the same seller can lower shipping and handling costs.

### ADDITIONAL TIPS:
• Ask for a bead count if the seller is offering items by the strand.

• Leave good feedback after a satisfactory transaction.

• Keep a list of your favorite online sellers.

### CAVEAT EMPTOR
When shopping the Web for that special bead, beware. Sellers on eBay should offer full descriptions of beads, including origin, quantity and size. If it seems too good to be true, it probably is. Be aware of the seller's shipping and handling charges. Sellers sometimes offer multiple items shipped together at no additional charge. While the charge may seem high for a single item, dividing the shipping may justify the cost.

# On the Web

*Sue Kwong and Karen Li: Arial's Gift.*

If you are in search of that special bead, be sure to look on the Web. The online retailers and the various Internet auction sites can be a valuable resource for inspiration and supplies. The Internet can help if you are not in an area with everything you need.

# Big-Box Craft Stores and Discount Stores

Some big-box craft stores have pre-packed beads (sometimes at exceptional value). The assortments can be limited, but if value is your goal, and you don't have a local bead shop in your area, give them a try. Previously it was difficult to find a good bead source, now the trouble is how to limit your selections!

# Magazines and Books

Bead magazines offer an astounding array of ads from people selling beads, either by catalog or online. Get copies of the latest beading magazines; you will find projects and advertisements from many suppliers who sell to the individual bead enthusiast. (See Resource Guide, page 214.)

*Bead magazines feature information on upcoming regional bead shows. The shows are organized like an open market, where you can see and purchase beads from a large number of vendors and artists. Check with the chapter of a local bead society for details.*

*Courtesy of Beadazzled. Photography by William L. Allen.*

# Your Jewelry Box

*Susan Ray: Amtrak West Ensemble.*

Don't forget to look for beads even closer to home, maybe in the closest jewelry box. Some unique pieces are probably hiding in Mom's or Grandma's jewelry box. With permission, of course, they may be just waiting for you to recycle them into a new creation.

**NOTE:** Be sure you are not cutting apart a priceless designer piece before beginning.

While you're at it, check your own jewelry box for outdated jewelry that you could take apart and use. You may find at least one or two necklaces or bracelets that you have not worn in years. They are just yearning to be reclaimed in a new creation.

## Vintage Shops

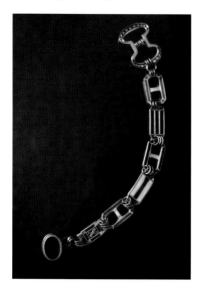

Jessica Italia: Buckle-Up Bracelet.
Courtesy of Galena Beads.

Jeanne Holland: Signature.
Courtesy of Vintaj Natural Brass Co.

Vintage pieces can be a great source for beautiful beads. The online auction sites also offer opportunities for you to buy vintage jewelry, sometimes at very good prices. If you don't already have vintage beads of your own, check out your local antiques shops and secondhand and resale stores. The stock is always changing, and you never know what you might find. (See Cleaning Your Beads and Findings, page 48.)

Vintaj Natural Brass Co. findings are perfect for creating vintage looks. (See Resource Guide, page 214.)

## Friends and Family

Beads are also fun to trade. Having some friends over to bead may start a ruckus as you swap beads back and forth. Don't be afraid to ask. We all have purchased beads and found that after making our delectable piece of jewelry, we have plenty of beads left over. Why not share them with a friend?

*Wendy Mullane: Artesian Willow Pond Necklace.*

*Susan A. Karczewski: Cut Glass Pendant and Earrings.*

# CLEANING YOUR BEADS AND FINDINGS

Although there are likely many ways to effectively clean beads, the options listed below are tried and true. Keep in mind that if you are reclaiming beads, you should cut them apart from the original strand before cleaning them.

*NOTE:* Be sure to know what you have before taking your scissors to your vintage strands.

**Mild Soap and Water:** Start with the least abrasive cleaner first. In this case, it is a mild soap (possibly dish soap) in lukewarm water. Allow the soap to dilute, then drop in your beads. After 15 minutes, check on your beads. If more cleansing is needed, gently agitate the water to bring bubbles back to the surface and continue to soak your beads. Some beads will need to be submerged overnight. If this method is not satisfactory, try dental tablets.

**Dental Tablets:** To clean loose beads, dental tablets work quite well. Drop your beads into a glass container with water, and then drop in a tablet. A few minutes later, you will have a lovely find. Test one bead before you immerse them all. Sometimes, beads have a reaction to the chemicals and will peel back. On those rare occasions, simply choose the mild soap and water solution.

**Glass Cleaner:** For glass beads, try a simple glass cleaner. Drop your separated beads into a plastic container. Add a mixture of three parts glass cleaner to two parts water and soak overnight. If the beads still need care the next morning, repeat the process with new glass cleaner and water. Again, test this process on a few beads beforehand. Sometimes, you may mistake acrylics for glass. Acrylics do not like glass cleaner at all and may turn cloudy, so be careful. Test first.

# CARING FOR CRYSTALS, NATURAL STONES AND PEARLS

Always wash your hands before working with your beads. Crystals especially need TLC when it comes to cleaning them or working them into a design. The oils from your hands can collect on the beads and make them dull. Crystals should be radiant. Treat them with special care. Commercial glass cleaner works exceptionally well for most crystal beads.

When transporting crystals or storing crystal jewelry pieces, separate them from other beads. The faceted edges of the crystals can be chipped or may scratch, whether in transport or just sitting side-by-side in a jewelry box.

Vintage crystals and gemstones can be especially delicate. When buying vintage crystals or gemstones, be sure to look at them under a loupe (a jeweler's eyepiece). You will find fractures and missing corners on those whose care was less than perfect.

Natural stones, freshwater pearls and crystals are also porous. Be sure to put them on after you use hairspray, perfume or nail polish remover, as each can damage bead finishes.

Gemstone jewelry should be stored in cloth bags. Gemstones are sensitive to heat and light and can easily be scratched by other jewelry.

*Sue Kwong and Karen Li: Signature Crystal Watch.*

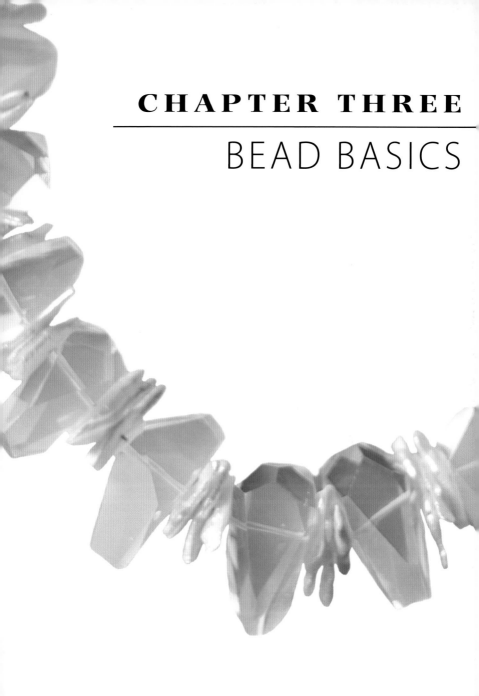

# CHAPTER THREE

## BEAD BASICS

*Courtesy of Galena Beads.*

## ALL ABOUT BEADS

*With Susan Ray and Sue Wilke*

Beads abound. Study their shapes, sizes and finishes. Many beads are priced based on their composition, origin and quality. Beads are described by their size, shape, texture, color, transparency, clarity and finish. Make a note of the country of origin. It is fun to use beads from faraway places.

Keep a journal. Chart your discoveries on a world map. You can involve your family in your beading expeditions and take a geographic and historic journey along the way.

Having trouble deciding on what beads to use? The knowledgeable staff at a specialty bead store will be glad to help you with your selection. Consider your lifestyle. If you are active

and energetic, you may want to stay away from beads that are especially fragile. Is a budget your concern? Express your wishes, and the specialty bead store will be able to assist.

Create a journal for record-keeping; use the sample chart on page 54 as a guide. Add your thoughts. Your personal entries will be a vivid reminder of the beads for years to come.

*Beading is a therapeutic hobby for all ages. It relaxes you and takes your mind off of the everyday stress you may encounter. Basically, anything with a hole in it is a bead. There are no rules to beading; you're the artist. You may enjoy using beads in numerous ways: stringing, linking, wrapping, coiling, braiding, winding and twisting. Believe me, there are many more! Beading is also a great learning technique for young children to develop their visual perception, practice sequencing and use basic math skills.*

*— Jessica Italia*

*Courtesy of Galena Beads.*

# BEAD JOURNAL CHART

| Location | Price | Qty. | Shape | Size | Color | Opacity | Texture | Origin |
|----------|-------|------|-------|------|-------|---------|---------|--------|
|          |       |      |       |      |       |         |         |        |
|          |       |      |       |      |       |         |         |        |
|          |       |      |       |      |       |         |         |        |
|          |       |      |       |      |       |         |         |        |
|          |       |      |       |      |       |         |         |        |
|          |       |      |       |      |       |         |         |        |
|          |       |      |       |      |       |         |         |        |
|          |       |      |       |      |       |         |         |        |
|          |       |      |       |      |       |         |         |        |
|          |       |      |       |      |       |         |         |        |
|          |       |      |       |      |       |         |         |        |
|          |       |      |       |      |       |         |         |        |
|          |       |      |       |      |       |         |         |        |
|          |       |      |       |      |       |         |         |        |
|          |       |      |       |      |       |         |         |        |
|          |       |      |       |      |       |         |         |        |
|          |       |      |       |      |       |         |         |        |
|          |       |      |       |      |       |         |         |        |
|          |       |      |       |      |       |         |         |        |
|          |       |      |       |      |       |         |         |        |
|          |       |      |       |      |       |         |         |        |
|          |       |      |       |      |       |         |         |        |
|          |       |      |       |      |       |         |         |        |
|          |       |      |       |      |       |         |         |        |
|          |       |      |       |      |       |         |         |        |
|          |       |      |       |      |       |         |         |        |
|          |       |      |       |      |       |         |         |        |

*Susan Ray: Semiprecious and Bone Lariat Necklace. The circle-shaped large pendant in the lariat is a common shape for semiprecious gemstones. The example shown is carnelian.*

# BEADS BY CATEGORIES

Here are some of the most popular beads used today:

## The Naturals, Pearls and Gemstones

Carried across the trade routes from the Far East, India and Africa, natural beads were probably the first beads ever worn. Natural beads include many types of shells: aba-lone, oyster, mother of pearl, freshwater pearls, carved and smooth bone, and wood.

*Susan Ray: Bear Claw Necklace.*

*Susan Ray: Five-Strand Basic Necklace. See Metal Clay, pages 86-87.*

*Courtesy of Beadazzled. Photography by William L. Allen.*

Gemstones include tigereye, hematite, jade, coral, black onyx, obsidian, fluorite, turquoise, goldstone, agate, jasper, quartz, aventurine, sodalite, serpentine, lapis lazuli and freshwater pearls, among others. Some of these beads have been carved into shapes unusual in other types of beads—especially jade and bone, which can be intricately carved with fine details.

Gemstones are also available in strands of chips. These chips are reasonably priced and can add texture to any design. Sometimes, beads resting on a bead board are not oriented properly and will actually take less room once strung. This especially happens with gemstone chips, which are odd shapes. At rest, the chips will appear to occupy more space than they actually do. So, measure twice and crimp once.

**BEAD INFLUENCES**

Amethyst = Love

Aventurine = Good Luck

Blue Gold = Calm

Crystal = Purity

Garnet = Romance

Jasper = Harmony

Multi = Unity

Rose Quartz = Balance

Sodalite = Tranquility

Tigereye = Peace

Turquoise = Healing

Unakite = Trust

*Sue Kwong/Karen Li: Flower Pendant Necklace.*

Newest among the naturals collection are flowers encased in an epoxy coating to keep the flower everlasting. (See Fire Mountain Gems, Resource Guide, page 214.)

*The true fascination of beads lies in their diversity. Beads are among the oldest human art forms, found in archaeological sites dating back tens of thousands of years. The rich diversity of beads comes from rocks and minerals, other natural materials of the earth and the handiwork of many cultures of the world.*

*— Jessica Italia*

## Pressed Glass

Glass beads originally were created to imitate the fabulous jewels of kings and queens. Pressed glass often is made through cottage industries and varies by maker. Offered in a wonderful variety of shapes, sizes and finishes, there are pressed glass beads for every jewelry designer's needs. These beads are available in rounds, ovals, bicones, rondelles, discs, flats, spirals, squared ovals, barrels, three-sided ovals, spirals, spears, crescents, moons, cubes, beehives, rice shapes, triangles, tubes, hearts, teardrops, stars, bell caps, flowers, grapes, leaves, fish, animal shapes, buttons, paddles and crows. Finishes include frosted satin and clear high-polished, as well as aurora borealis and vitriol finishes, to name just a few. Among pressed glass beads there are selections of alphabet and numbered beads. Other types of pressed glass recently imported from China include beads with transparent layers over colored or foil inner beads, as well as crackled-glass beads.

*Jessica Tracey: Be Happy Necklace.*

*Sue Wilke: Memory Wire Provence Rhapsody.*

### HOW MANY BEADS DO YOU NEED?

*A simple way to figure out how many beads your necklace will require is to take a sampling of the beads you are planning to use and line them up on your bead board. Divide the number 4 into your desired finished length. Cover a 4" length. Count the number of beads that will be required to cover this 4". Then multiply your number of beads by the finished length of the necklace or bracelet.*

*Example: If it takes 12 beads to fill the 4" length and you want your finished necklace to be 16", divide 16" by 4 (equals 4) and then multiply 12 by 4 for an outcome of 48 beads needed to complete your piece.*

*Use your bead board! The board offers accurate measurements for multiple necklaces and it allows you to change bead order or change the type of beads used without disturbing your design work.*

*The numbers of beads you will need per inch, based on bead size:*

*4mm = 6.25 beads*
*6mm = 4.25 beads*
*8mm = 3.25 beads*
*10mm = 2.50 beads*
*12mm = 2.00 beads*

*Example: For 16" of size 12mm beads: 2.00 x 16 = 32 beads*

### BEADS BY WEIGHT GUIDE

*Some beads are measured by weight and because beads are sold internationally, many sellers will refer to them in the metric system:*

*28 grams is equal to 1 ounce*

*100 grams is equal to 3.56 ounces*

*448 grams is equal to 1 pound*

*½ kilo is equal to 500 grams (1.1 lbs.)*

*1 kilo is equal to 1000 grams (2.2 lbs.)*

## Lamp Beads

Described as "lamp beads" or "furnace" glass, these beads generally are mass-produced glass beads (many made in China or India) that have certain characteristics of fine artist "lampwork" beads. If you are unfamiliar with the differences, ask your local specialty store to show them to you. Compare their luminosity, their quality and their smoothness with that of fine, hand-made lampwork beads. It will be easy to tell, once you have seen the differences for yourself. The more familiar you become with quality beads, the easier it will be for you to discern value when making purchases.

## Art Glass or Lampwork Beads

Prized for centuries for their artisan style, lampwork beads are made on the torch of an experienced lampwork artist. They are simply irresistible.

See Creating Lampwork Beads with Karen Leonardo, page 100 for more about lampwork.

*Michelle McKenzie: Turquoise Series. Courtesy of McKenzie Glassworks.*

## Jet

While the Civil War raged, other parts of the world mourned the loss of Queen Victoria's husband, Prince Albert. To show their respect, ladies of that day wore jewelry made of jet. Jet is one of the oldest natural materials used for beads as a product of a fossilized tree from the Jurassic period. Today, glass bead makers mimic the beautiful and often-faceted jet with that of shiny black glass.

*Karen Leonardo: Peacock Drury Lampwork Necklace.*

## Cut Crystal

Crystal is available from a number of regions throughout the world: Czech Republic, Austria, Germany and China. Crystal is also available in a number of shapes, including: rounds, drops, ovals, rondelles, bicones and hearts, among others. Crystal also is available in transparent, as well as opaque, finishes.

Cut crystal is faceted. Fancy finishes include aurora borealis, vitriol or rainbow-like and gold- or bronze-coated. Colors often imitate gemstones: sapphire, emerald, topaz, ruby, peridot, diamond, amethyst, labradorite and many other colors. With today's technology, colors are often available

*Sue Kwong/Karen Li: Signature Cut Crystal Necklace.*

in many shades, as well. Blue, for example, comes in shades of aqua, turquoise, light sapphire and sapphire. Study any number of mail-order bead catalogs. They offer a good sampling of the most popular beads and crystals and will give you an idea of the range of colors and shapes available.

# Fire-Polished Glass

Fire-polished glass has a similar look and feel to cut-crystal beads but is usually less expensive. Because fire-polished beads are mass produced, they are widely available. These beads are also offered in unusual finishes, including two tones and coatings similar to those used with seed beads.

Fire-polished beads may not have the luminosity of fine-cut crystal beads, but if your budget is limited, they are an excellent alternative and will also glisten. Look for a wide variety of shapes and finishes. Favorite fire-polished glass beads include "cathedral" faceted beads. These beads vary slightly from vendor to vendor but are generally oval, faceted beads that have gold- or silver-tone ends that are tapered. These beads look vintage and go well with a variety of other beads, including pearls. The shapes are so diverse it would be difficult to list all of them here. They include rounds, ovals, drops, tri-sliced, windows and barrels, among others.

*Courtesy of Galena Beads.*

**DID YOU KNOW?**

*Glass of antiquity can be found in many museum collections. See our information on the Bead Museum in Washington, D.C., and the Bead Timeline, page 23. Or read Lois Sherr Dubin's remarkable book,* **The History of Beads,** *for further study.*

Courtesy of Beadazzled. Photography by William L. Allen.

## Seed Beads

Seed beads are probably familiar to you from your days in summer camp. Often chosen for small projects, seed beads frequently are introduced with the use of a small loom. But don't let that first experience dissuade you from using them. Seed beads are definitely for adults, too! I am amazed not only by their variety in size, color and finish, but also by how such a tiny bead can have such a great impact in a design.

You will find many examples of the uses of seed beads in this book, but still other examples exist. Seed beads are used in embroidery and for amulets, pouches, bead sculptures and fringe. The beads are also popular for bead landscapes in traditional applications, like peyote stitches and brick stitches, as well as free-form contemporary work. (See Stitchery, pages 152- 199.)

Cindy Yost and Kat Allison: Earthy Denim Bracelet.

Seed beads are offered in more than 4,000 colors and finishes and are also identified by cut: rocailles, three-cuts, two-cuts, drops, true-cuts, bugle beads, maco tubes, unicas and Japanese Miyuki Delicas. You can often buy seed beads by half-kilos, kilos and sometimes by the pound. Seed beads are also available in a variety of sizes from 1/0 rocailles to 15/0 true-cuts.

*Sometimes, seed beads are sold by mass. A mass is 1,200 beads. A hank is usually 12 or 14 strands that are 12" to 16" long. Check before buying. Not only does the number of strands vary, the length of the strands can vary dramatically as well. Vintage lengths are often much shorter. Once you begin to find vendors you like, you will become familiar with their methods of measurement and be comfortable buying beads from them.*

*Cindy Yost and Kat Allison: Copper on Blue Bracelet.*

## TRY THESE EXERCISES TO SEE THE SEED BEAD IMPACT ON YOUR DESIGNS

**Exercise One:**

Select three sets of 12 beads from 6mm to 20mm in size that have a similar theme or colorway. Add three different strands of seed beads in very different finishes and colors to the first three sets. String the 12 beads using the seed beads as spacers. Look at the difference the diversity offers. Try varying the number of seed beads used as spacers. Did you like one, three or twelve seed beads between each bead? Mix the various seed beads and string one of the pieces again. Do you like the new mix of seed beads with your design? Vary the pattern. String the seed beads sequentially and try another section with randomly strung colors. You will soon find the power of the tiny bead in the palms of your hands.

*Susan Ray: Rocky Mountain Journey.*

**Exercise Two:**

String a strand of beads for a bracelet, but do not attach to a clasp yet. Combine one strand of seed beads and one or two styles of the common beads in the bracelet for the second strand. String 8 to 14 seed beads, and then insert one of your common beads. Continue until you have the proper length. Repeat for strand three. Place the three strands together. See how easy it is to make a multi-strand bracelet using the addition of seed beads?

## Bugles

Bugles are classified as a category of seed beads. They have sharp edges that can cut some types of stringing materials. Experts sometimes use clear nail polish on the edges to prevent the edges from fraying thread.

## Porcelain and Ceramic

*Sandi Webster: Rio Necklace.*

Porcelain beads start as fine clays, often made in molds that are hand painted in their bisque stage and then fired using glazing techniques. Since they are hand painted, their designs may vary. Ceramic beads can be carved and/or hand painted. Many ceramic beads retain their primitive characteristics and are left in their natural, matte-clay finish.

## Specialty Beads

Fiber optics are among the many new and exciting specialty beads technology has made available. They resemble tigereyes and are available in many colors, shapes and sizes. Also, miracle beads have reflecting layers that give the illusion of depth.

## Acrylics

Today's technology allows acrylics to imitate many of the basic bead types. Discerning the differences can require more than hitting the bead against the plate enamel of your teeth (as some veterans will tell you is a tried-and-true test). Experience will be your best guide as to whether a bead is authentic or an impersonator. The one drawback of acrylics is that some dull over time, reclaiming that "oily" finish from their origin. Even specialty cleaners can't undo their intrinsic nature. However, acrylic beads offer a wide variety of beads at very reasonable prices. So, if you are working on a fashion-fad piece, and you can get the look you want with acrylics, don't hesitate to give them a try. They will be easy on your pocketbook, too.

# Metal Beads and Findings

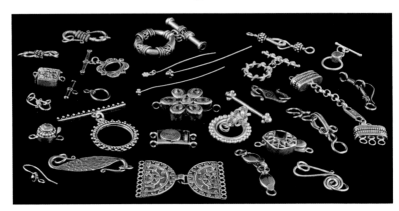

*Courtesy of Beadazzled. Photography by William L. Allen.*

Precious metal beads and findings are available in sterling silver, pewter, gold and gold-filled varieties. They are available in numerous fashion shapes and sizes. Many are stamped with designs or intricately cut out. Metal beads can also be made by electroplating sterling, gold or copper to base metals (including natural and man-made materials). These beads and findings have luminous finishes

*Courtesy of Galena Beads.*

resembling precious metals that will not peel away and are usually less expensive. Pewter is a soft metal, so if you choose to use pewter beads or findings, be sure they will not be placed under stress in your design. Pewter clasps are not recommended, as they often are too soft and will sometimes break apart.

*Jessica Italia: Crimson Lights.*

# Vintage Beads

*Jeanne Holland: Classic Cabbage Rose Choker.*

Another good source for beads may be as close as your community thrift store. Old necklaces, bracelets, earrings and pendants are excellent sources to help fill a beginner's bead box or add spice to your own collections. Have a look at your local thrift shop or antique mall. You may find a true gem.

Clean your beads carefully with soap and water. Always check to be sure you are not cutting apart a priceless treasure. You will see some fine examples of designs made from "newly created" vintage findings by Vintaj Natural Brass Co. later on in this book. (See pages 148 and 159.)

# Bead Sizes

Metric is the name of the game when it comes to beads. Beads come from all over the world, and because the metric system is used elsewhere, beads are measured in millimeters more often than not. If you never were a fan of metrics, here are simple charts to help you make the transition. Be sure to keep your chart handy when buying beads online. Photos can distort the size of a bead. Be sure to read the fine print when buying beads online or in catalogs.

Beads by Weight Guide, page 60.

*As you touch and feel the textures, a whole new meaning and understanding comes over you. An array of cultures, religions and politics have a distinct presence. A way of life for so many societies is expressed through beads marking marriage and major achievements. Traded as means of currency through the ages, beads are 30,000 years of thoughts, passions and dreams.*

*— Jessica Italia*

*Courtesy of Galena Beads.*

# BEAD SIZE CHART

**NOTE:** These are actual size.

## Millimeter/Inch Gauge

| mm | inches |
|---|---|
| 0mm | 0 |
| | ¼ |
| 10mm | ½ |
| 20mm | ¾ |
| | 1 |
| 30mm | |

## Bugle Bead Sizes

1   2   3   5

## Size

7/0 ⊚ ☐☐☐☐☐☐☐☐☐☐
8/0 ⊚ ☐☐☐☐☐☐☐☐☐☐☐☐
9/0 ⊚ ☐☐☐☐☐☐☐☐☐☐☐☐
10/0 ⊚ ☐☐☐☐☐☐☐☐☐☐☐☐☐
11/0 ⊚ ☐☐☐☐☐☐☐☐☐☐☐☐☐
12/0 ⊚ ☐☐☐☐☐☐☐☐☐☐☐☐☐☐
14/0 ⊚ ☐☐☐☐☐☐☐☐☐☐☐☐☐☐☐
16/0 ⊙ ☐☐☐☐☐☐☐☐☐☐☐☐☐☐☐☐
20/0 · ☐☐☐☐☐☐☐☐☐☐☐☐☐☐☐☐☐

## Square mm Sizes

3 x 3 mm ■
4 x 4 mm ■
5 x 5 mm ■

## Seed Beads Per Inch

Use these approximate counts of seed beads per inch to help plan your own designs

| Bead Size | Beads Per Inch |
|---|---|
| 11/0 | 20 |
| 8/0 | 12 |
| 5/0 | 7 |

## Oval Bead Sizes in Millimeters

6 x 4
7 x 5
8 x 6
10 x 8
12 x 10
14 x 10
16 x 12

## Round Bead Sizes in Millimeters

2mm •
3mm •
4mm ●
5mm ●
6mm ●
7mm ●
8mm ●
9mm ●
10mm ●
11mm ●
12mm ●
14mm ●
16mm ●
18mm ●

# CHAPTER FOUR

## GETTING IT TOGETHER

## ORGANIZATION

When you bring home your first
beads, spread them out to admire
them. You will marvel at the array of
beautiful colors, textures and sizes,
as well as how they capture the light.
How should you store these treasures?
From your first purchases to your ever-
expanding collection, there are plenty
of options for storing your beads.
Choose what's right for you.

### Storing Your Beads

Be sure that your beads, supplies and
tools are stored in a safe, dry place. They
should be easily accessible to your workspace. Organize! Beads and tools are
compact and easy to store, but organization is a must. Have a dedicated space
for your hobby. With organized materials
at hand, you will be able to spend more
time enjoying beading rather than
searching for what you need.

*Small zip-closure bags are a great way
to sort beads for projects. They also
layer nicely into a flat, clear box, making
it easy to see what is inside without
opening the lids. If you sort lampwork
beads by artist, put each in a separate
container, you can quickly pick the focal
inspiration for your next project.*

*—Sue Wilke*

### FINDING TIME FOR "MOMENTS OF INSPIRATION"

*Crunched for time? How often have you felt creative, only to think, "I just don't have the time." Here are a few tips so you can create a few moments of inspiration. Despite our jobs or caring for our children, all of us have a couple of minutes that we can use to be inspired. You just need to have your tools at hand when these "windows of opportunity" open.*

• *Take time during your coffee break, at your lunch hour, when your kids are at sports practice or even waiting for the spin cycle to let your ideas take shape.*

• *Get containers to keep all of your tools at hand and your projects together. You can then put them in the car or the stroller and you are set.*

• *There are many craft totes on the market, or use a tackle box or a makeup case. Even a lunch box would do the trick. You will also need some small containers to hold your collection of beads.*

• *A bead mat and/or a bead board are a must so your project doesn't roll around.*

• *Keep a small notebook handy to jot down ideas for future projects whever — and wherever — inspiration strikes.*

• *Having moments of inspiration to look forward to each day will make even the most stressful day enjoyable.*

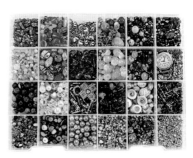

Keep your beads stored by color. It really makes finding a bead of the right color quick and easy.

**NOTE:** Be sure to keep beads away from small children. The colors and shapes may fool a child into thinking they are candy, so do keep them out of sight and on a shelf high enough to be out of the reach of small children.

*Beads can be hazardous to your pets. Keep beading and stringing materials out of their reach. If you have cats, it's a good idea to cover your work area with a bath towel or blanket. If you are beading and get called away, then just cover your whole work area with the blanket to prevent any unwanted alterations to your progress.*

# Setting Up Your Space

Choose a workspace and arrangement that is comfortable for you. You hear a lot about ergonomics these days, and those concerns are well-founded when beading. Because beading can be consuming, you may be sitting longer than you realize. Move and stretch periodically, and practice these ergonomic fine points:

• Choose a table or desk with a chair that is the correct height for you. This is essential.

• Get a work surface that is large enough to lay out your bead board, tools and bead box.

• Very good lighting is critical. A portable, true-color lamp is an excellent choice. It shows the colors and details of the beads, works great for color matching, and reduces eye fatigue.

*Jessica Italia: Santa Fe Bracelet.*

*Courtesy of Beadazzled. Photography by Cas Webber.*

## TAKE IT WITH YOU

Many art stores carry a variety of suitable, portable, craft totes for your beading tools and supplies. Tackle or portable toolbox-type totes are very handy. They can hold small bead containers as well as trays and stringing supplies. Some rip-stop nylon totes are designed to hold the plastic divided-container boxes.

*Always look for plastic storage containers with dividers that are permanently affixed and a lid that closes flush with the top of the dividers. This way, when the unit is raised for carrying, no beads will migrate and mix.*

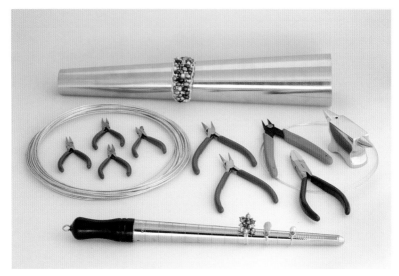

*Courtesy of Beadazzled. Photography by William L. Allen.*

# BASIC TOOLBOX
## Tools to Have on Hand

- Wire cutters
- Flat- or chain-nose pliers
- Needle-nose or round-nose pliers
- Journal for inspiration
- Colored pencils
- Bead board and/or bead mat
- Plastic container for honey pot; see page 80
- Muffin tin or other sorting cups (like an ice cube tray)
- True-color light (optional but a good value)
- Various glues (E6000 is a great jewelry glue)

- Tweezers
- Crimping pliers
- Anvil
- Chasing hammer
- Stringing materials
- Ruler
- Beading needle
- Ring sizer (optional)
- Bracelet form (optional)
- Bead cement (optional)

*Choosing the right set of tools checklist:*

- *Buy the best tools you can afford.*

- *Look for an ergonomic tool set (see Resource Guide, page 214) and a comfortable fit in your hand.*

- *Get textured or padded handles to prevent slipping.*

- *Remember you are working on jewelry, not building a house, so look for tools that have small enough blades for extremely detailed work.*

- *Check the strength of the blades (use cutters only to their maximum cutting capacity).*

- *Tungsten carbide or titanium blades are more durable than alloys.*

- *Antiglare finish will prevent eye fatigue.*

- *Spring tension supplies extended support.*

- *Resistance to rust is useful if you live in a humid climate.*

- *Add a protective, rubberized coating to the tips of your pliers, following the manufacturer's directions. The coating will prevent your pliers from scratching the filigree's finish.*

## CUTTERS

Cutters are used to cut flexible wire. They have very sharp blades.

***NOTE:*** Never use scissors to cut flexible wire. Use a wire cutter and keep it safe in your toolbox, away from hubby and kids.

## FLAT-NOSE PLIERS

These pliers are reliable for crimping beads. Look for short jaws that are designed for delicate work. Tapered points help in getting to tight spots. Never use serrated jaws.

*Although crimping pliers are available, flattening a crimp with flat-nose pliers has proven consistently more reliable for me.*

## ROUND-NOSE PLIERS

Round-nose pliers, also known as chain-nose pliers, are used to create loops for earrings, dangles and spirals. Never use serrated jaws that can mar your finding's surface.

## THE HONEY POT

*Several varieties of honey pots.*

A honey pot is a container you can use to collect a number of styles, shapes, colors and sizes of beads for use in a project. Any container will do, but clear colorless plastic works best. This avoids the risk of the color of the container influencing your assortment. Plastic ware is a good choice. A lid also helps with portability.

**Sue Wilke's Honey Pot Method:**
Fabulous combinations of beads can be found by sorting sizes, colors and shapes that are compatible into a container, and then randomly laying handfuls of beads in whatever order they appear.

This technique is so rewarding, especially when it is a little late in the evening and you want to bead for enjoyment. There is little counting or sorting. It is fast and safe — and relaxing, since little thinking is involved. After you work with beads for a while, you come to love certain fill beads. There are certain beads that I use over and over. You will come to know what pleases you by simple experimentation.

## MUFFIN TIN
After you have finished a project, return your beads to their rightful "homes." A muffin tin makes the sorting simple, and your task will be done quickly. Try sorting beads while on the phone with a friend or watching TV to take the "task" out of the job.

## BEAD BOARDS

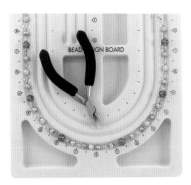

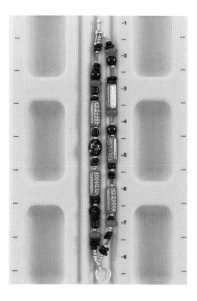

Bead boards are available in a number of materials and widths. Some bead boards have separate areas to sort beads and findings. Many boards have more than one channel so that you can comfortably work on more than one strand of your project at once. Most bead boards have rulers. The three- and four-channel trays provide a wide variety of uses, but always use the outermost channel when making a one-strand bracelet or necklace. The channels closer to the middle of the board are not as accurate. They work fine when reducing lengths for multi-strands, but can be deceptive for work on a single-strand piece.

Flocked boards are excellent for holding beads in place. If you get the urge to bead and your tray is not with you, use a terry cloth towel or a piece of fleece to lay out beads. The nap of the cloth will hold the beads in place.

### VARIOUS GLUES

Some projects require glue. E6000 is a highly recommended jewelry and craft glue. Also, be sure to have a quick-drying glue handy.

# BEGINNER'S PRACTICE

Lay out a row of beads in the first channel. Use the "0" on the ruler (at the bottom of the board) as your center. Place beads on either side of the "0." You may choose to do either a symmetrical or an asymmetrical pattern. Lay beads in place as inspiration suggests.

If you are planning to add seed beads to your creation, there is no need to lay them out on the board first, unless your design requires much attention. Figure up the number of seed beads required for your overall design and leave enough room to accommodate their insertion. (See the Seed Bead Chart on page 71.)

"Inspiration is about vision, sparks of insight, and the passionate desire to create. Realizing the vision, however, requires disciplined practice, leading to dexterity, and eventually, virtuosity, in the chosen medium. As the musician endlessly practices scales until her fingers can reproduce on her instrument the melodies in her heart, the beader usually starts with simple patterns, moving on as her skills expand, until she begins solving design challenges in new ways. Inspiration is the jumping-off point into the ocean of our own imaginations. The creative response may be evoked by an unexpected color harmony in nature; a tribal costume; an exotic architectural detail; or the provocative juxtaposition of components of different eras, cultures or materials. Whatever wakes up our creative instinct, ignites our desire to express our own visions."

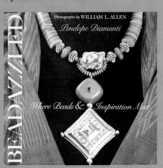

Reproduced with permission from *Beadazzled, from* Where Beads and Inspiration Meet *by Penelope Diamanti. Beadazzled, 2006.*

# Time to Try a Design of Your Own

Choose beads of varied sizes, shapes, textures, sheens, transparencies and color, to fill in your creation. Varying size, shapes, textures and more can add complexity to the work without learning any fancy stringing techniques. Also, varying the color and transparency can heighten or soften a design's appearance. Larger or brighter beads add movement and electricity to the pattern. Experiment. You will wear your piece of jewelry many, many times, so a little extra time spent choosing your pattern now can make quite a difference.

Relax! There is no right or wrong. Jewelry is such fun to make and wear. Because a piece can be finished in as little as 30 minutes, it provides almost instant gratification. So, give it a whirl. And don't forget to breathe. Beading is actually very tranquil and lets you give pause to a hurried world.

*Your first design effort may not be totally unencumbered. Realize this is your first piece, and you are taking "baby steps" to becoming the jewelry artist you wish to be. You will be back for more, and next time with much less trepidation about it.*

*When beginning your project, try several arrangements of beads. Once you have an assortment of 20 to 30 beads (average size approximately 6mm) for your bracelet, or 60 or more for a necklace, begin to lay your beads into a channel on the bead board. If you require a few more beads, you can easily return to your bead box. Some bead designers will string several repetitions of patterns to see how the design will look when strung. If you are having trouble visualizing the project from the bead board, try this method, as follows.*

*1. Cut 12" of flexible wire.*

*2. Place a knot at one end.*

*3. String one seed bead as a stopper, and then string several repetitions of your design.*

*Sometimes it's easier to begin when you can "see" your beads already strung.*

# CHAPTER FIVE

## MAKING BEADS

# METAL CLAY

*With Susan Ray*

*Lynn Larkin: Silver Spirals Necklace.*

In recent years, metal clay has been introduced to this country. This new medium has led to the creation of individual silver and/or gold beads and pendants of very fine quality. Although metal clay, like lampwork, can require a kiln, the newest versions of the clay allow you to fire a small bead or pendant using a small butane torch and a firing stone. Many companies now offer a reasonable introductory kit for your use. (See Fire Mountain Gems, Resource Guide, page 214.)

The new low-fire versions of metal clay have provided an easy and relatively inexpensive entry into this medium. A dehydrator can be the best way to dry the clay, which must be totally dry before firing. In little time, you can design a piece of metal clay, dry it, fire it and create a substantial piece of jewelry. See Silver Metal Clay Pendant designed by Susan Ray, page 104.

Although this product is called "clay," it does not yet present the flexible and elastic qualities of a polymer. Also, the clay begins to dry immediately when you open the package, which doesn't allow much time to "play" with it. I prefer to create flexible molds, using Polyform's Sculpey MoldMaker & Polymer Clay Conditioner for fast-release molds. Once the molds are designed and baked, they become one of the easiest methods to use with metal clay. Open the metal clay package (follow all manufacturer's directions). Tear a piece of clay approximately the size of the finished piece you are planning, and push it into the mold. The Mold-Maker captures texture well, and luckily, so does the metal clay, so the mold will give me a good transfer. Give the newly created piece plenty of time to dry.

Sculpey and other companies also produce clay texture sheets (which resemble rubber stamps without the wood-block backing) to create additional textures on your metal or polymer clay, if you do not want to take the time to create your own.

There are many techniques available to finish your clay piece. Immersing the fired and cooled clay design into liver of sulphur will turn the piece from an orange-brown to a black. Using a good silver polish and elbow grease, you can polish the high spots, and the design will retain the darkened appearance within. This will give the piece an antique appearance.

# POLYMER CLAY

*With Susan Ray*

Polymer clay is available by a variety of makers. Clays from different manufacturers will vary. Some are more flexible; some are harder when baked.

You will need to experiment with the different clays to know which clay works best for you. Always follow manufacturer's directions for conditioning and baking your clay. Designate your tools, work surface, toaster oven and pasta machine for clay work only. Never re-use these items in your kitchen for food preparation.

Polymer clay is limited only by your imagination. It is an easy medium to work with, and it offers a vast array of colors. Polymer clay readily will pick up textures from rubber stamps. Its versatility is endless!

*Jessica Italia: Where Have All the Cowboys Gone? Bracelet.*

# SUSAN RAY'S SKEWER BEADS

*Susan Ray: "Magic" Paths.*

## CREATING SKEWER POLYMER BEADS

Skewer beads are made two ways: the Lump Method or Slab Method. For beginners, the Lump Method is a good starting point. Once you get the concept, you will want the additional control you get from the Slab Method. Polymer canes used in these techniques were supplied by Tracy Callahan.

Now it's time to build your skills by starting on a project.

## LUMP-METHOD SKEWER BEADS

### Supplies

½ ounce of any color of Sculpey Premo! Polymer Clay

Wooden skewer

Plastic work sheet (dedicated to polymer clay)

Flat blade cutter

Pasta machine (dedicated to polymer clay)

Toaster oven (dedicated to polymer clay)

*Optional: Sculpting tool with wooden handle*

*Optional: Extra-large emery board*

*Optional: Sculpey Satin or Gloss Glaze*

See The Clay Store, Resource Guide, page 214.

*Susan Ray's Skewer Beads.*
*Canes by Tracy Callahan.*

*I created this technique myself. I am sure that the idea originated in my mother's kitchen at some time or another, but for now, polymer is the medium!*

## TASK 1: MAKE A SKEWER BEAD

**Step A:** To create your first skewer base, take a lump of clay that is approximately ½ ounce in weight. It doesn't matter what color you use.

**Step B:** Condition the clay following the manufacturer's directions.

*Don't shortcut conditioning. Your beads will not harden if the clay is not properly conditioned. The polymer compounds need to be mixed before baking to allow the clay to harden to the proper consistency, so knead away!*

*Many polymer artists set aside time to "condition" clay by rolling it over and over through their pasta machines and then placing it in plastic bags for use when their creative juices are flowing.*

**Step C:** Roll the clay between your hands until it resembles a barrel shape approximately ½" in diameter and 1½" in length.

**Step D:** Place the skewer through the middle of the clay's short end.

**Step E:** Pull the lump to the middle of the skewer, being careful to keep the skewer in the center of the clay.

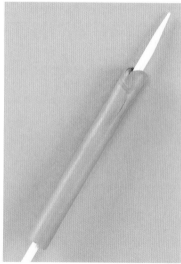

**Step F:** Try to retain the barrel shape as you move the clay up the skewer.

**Step G:** Now roll the clay on the skewer as you would roll out clay to make a snake. Use a clean, dry work surface that is dedicated to your polymer work. My work surface is an old Tupperware pie crust rolling mat.

*Never use your kitchen utensils, oven or supplies when working with polymer clay. Always have a separate set of tools just for clay work.*

**Step H:** Make the clay at least twice the length of the original, at least ¼" in diameter and 7" in length by rolling it along the work surface. Apply even pressure.

**Step I:** If the clay wall becomes too thin to work with (you must maintain at least ⅛" in thickness for beads), use your thumbs and forefingers to draw the clay back toward the center of the skewer and simply re-roll it.

**Step J:** Allow your new tube of beads to rest before cutting. I usually wait at least one hour.

*After you have used the skewer a few times, it will be coated with some of the polymer clay and the beads will no longer easily pull away from the skewer surface. Once this happens, you should discard the skewer and start anew.*

## TASK 2: CUTTING YOUR BEADS

**Step A:** For this first example we will use a ruler as the mark to cut the beads. Lay down your skewer next to a ruler edge and place a small slice (using your blade cutter) across the top of the skewered snake at each 1" mark. Now place the skewer in one hand, and using your blade cutter, complete the cut. It is helpful to start at one end.

**Step B:** Rotate the skewer and the clay to get an even cut all the way around. This takes some practice. Don't be discouraged if your first cuts are uneven. Using your blade, simply even up the ends. The beads may not all be a consistent size at this stage, but, hey, you made a very fine bead, didn't you?

**Step C:** Once the first bead is cut, remove it from the skewer, and tap each end onto the flat side of the blade cutter. This will help to even out your cut and give the ends a flat, consistent and professional appearance. Check for bad cuts. Sometimes a small sliver of clay will remain that needs attention. Simply massage it back into the clay body or cut it away. (If at first you don't succeed, remove your clay from the skewer and start again.) Now we're having fun!

**Step D:** You also can create a slight "well" in the ends of the bead by using a sculpting tool. Remove a bead from the skewer. Take your sculpting tool and place one end in the hole of the bead. Apply ever-so-slight pressure on the end, and the well will form naturally as the wooden handle of the tool meets the clay.

## TASK 3: BAKING AND FINISHING YOUR BEADS

**Step A:** Once all of the beads are cut to perfection, you are ready to bake them following manufacturer's directions. I use Sculpey Premo! clay exclusively and prefer to bake my beads in a toaster oven at 275 degrees for 20 to 30 minutes, depending on their size. You can place your beads directly onto the toaster oven pan or suspend them on a bicycle spoke. Either method works well.

**Step B:** Allow your beads to cool in the oven.

**Step C:** Sometimes, a shiny edge will appear where the clay touched the pan, or you may wish to add a glaze finish to your beads. If desired, use an emery board to clean up the beads. Left unglazed, most polymer beads will remain in their natural, soft-shine state.

> *I recommend buying some extra large emery boards from your local discount store. These are simple and easy to use. I often sit with a pot of beads in my lap while watching television and sand them to a fine finish using an emery board.*

**Step D:** If you want to add more shine to your beads, apply finishing glaze as directed by the manufacturer.

*Susan Ray: Gold Leaf Pendant Drop Necklace.*

## SLAB-METHOD SKEWER BEADS

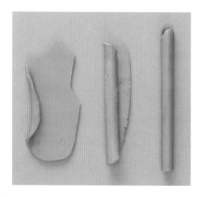

The slab method for making skewer beads takes a little more time, but it provides better control of the diameter of the beads.

### TASK 1: CREATE THE BEAD

**Step A:** Begin with a lump of clay that is approximately ½ ounce in weight.

**Step B:** Set your pasta machine on the thickest setting.

**Step C:** Condition the clay by rolling it through the pasta machine at least 15 times. Be sure to check manufacturer's directions regarding conditioning. Each clay body must be conditioned.

**Step D:** Continue to fold the clay in half, inserting the folded edge first through the machine until you have created a 2" x 4" slab.

**Step E:** Lay the wooden skewer lengthwise over one edge of the clay. Roll the clay onto the skewer to create the snake. Gently tap the seam into place.

**Step F:** Roll the clay out on your work sheet as stated in Task 1, Step G through Step J, on page 90.

See The Clay Store, Resource Guide, page 214.

### ADDING EMBELLISHMENTS

Roll the skewered clay through glitter or herbs to add inclusions or, make interesting color-combination canes. Just slice off the thinnest cane and apply to the skewer clay. Once you are happy with your inclusions, simply roll gently along your work surface. Use of inclusions is fun. Be safe, too! Some inclusions may be flammable. Take care to use only items that will not start a fire when you bake your beads in your toaster oven. Always — safety first.

Canes by Tracy Callahan*.

Pendant made with cane skewer beads, metal tube inclusions and clay canes by Tracy Callahan.

# AUTUMN POLYMER CLAY BEADS

*With Sheila Hobson*

*Sheila Hobson: Autumn Polymer Clay and Copper Bangle. Courtesy of Ebb Designs.*

**Designer:** Sheila Hobson, Ebb Designs
**Finished Size:** 8½"
**Expense:** Less than $25
**Expertise:** Intermediate
**Time to Complete:** A day

**Gathering Your Goods**
Premo! Polymer Clay: 2 oz. each of red, green, yellow and copper. You will use one-fourth to one-half of each package.

**Where to Find:** Artisans

**Tools to Have on Hand:**
Toothpick or skewer
Toaster oven (optional)
Pasta machine

## TASK 1: CONDITIONING YOUR CLAY

*Sheila Hobson, courtesy of Ebb Designs.
Photography by Ebb Designs.*

**Step A:** Condition the clay following the manufacturer's directions and make six triangles: two red, two green, two yellow.

**Step B:** Run the copper clay through the No. 5 pasta machine setting, and make two rectangles.

**Step C:** Blend the clay in two separate groups of triangles. Stack the rectangles, one on top of the other: red, copper, green, yellow and then yellow, green, copper and red. The copper rectangles should not overpower the other colors.

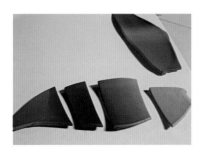

**Step D:** Separate the colors when finished. You should have blends of reds, greens, browns and yellows.

## TASK 2: CREATING YOUR BEADS

**Step A:** Use the blends to make 11 beads that progress from greens to reds. Also make a pile of 3mm beads in a progression of the blended colors.

**Step B:** Make three 6mm red beads and three 6mm green.

**Step C:** Make one 10mm red bead and one 10mm green.

**Step D:** Make one 13mm red bead and one 13mm green. Make one red or green 16mm bead.

*Sheila Hobson. Courtesy of Ebb Designs.*
*Photography by Ebb Designs.*

**Step E:** Embellish these beads by pressing on a progression of the 3mm beads you made in Task 2, Step A. Begin one end with greens and progress to the reds.

*Sheila Hobson. Courtesy of Ebb Designs.*

*Sheila Hobson. Courtesy of Ebb Designs.*
*Photography by Ebb Designs.*

**Step F:** Use a skewer or toothpick to create a bead hole in each bead. Vary your bead styles. Clay is so much fun! Fire the beads following manufacturer's directions.

# CREATING LAMPWORK BEADS

*With Karen Leonardo*

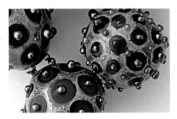

*Michelle McKenzie: Reduction bead.*
*Courtesy of McKenzie Glassworks.*

Dreaming about making your own lampwork beads?

Lampwork beads are handmade glass beads crafted by melting glass onto stainless steel rods. Today, many fine books offer valuable instructions, and expose the once-secretive methods of creating beautiful glass lampwork beads.

Basic glass bead-making starter kits ($100-$500) are available through many art glass suppliers. The kit will include: glass rods, a small gas torch, mandrels, bead release, eye protection and some lampworking tools. You must anneal (slow cool) your beads over

*Designer lampwork beads may be more difficult to find locally — try your favorite specialty bead store — and can be more expensive than the mass-market copies craft stores offer. Handmade lampwork is unique and often only one-of-a-kind is available. You will easily find lampwork online at auctions and at many artists' Web sites. Use your favorite online search engine to hunt for "lampwork" or "glass beads." Study bead magazines. Many artists and distributors advertise in Bead & Button, Beadwork, Lapidary Journal, Bead Style and Art Jewelry, as well as other bead magazines.*

many hours to reduce the potential for cracking or breakage. A slow cooker and vermiculite or a fiber blanket will suffice for the beginner. Using a specialty bead annealer or kiln will make this process simpler and more reliable. Follow proper guides for ventilation. Be sure to anchor your torch and have your tools placed so that you do not need to "cross" the flame to use them. As always, follow manufacturer's instructions for use, as well as safety, health and fire precautions. Keep a fire extinguisher available. Never leave your torch unattended.

*Karen Leonardo: Fuchsia Druzy Lampwork and Necklace Design.*

*Michelle McKenzie: Frit Bead.*
*Courtesy of McKenzie Glassworks.*

Begin by melting glass rods with the torch onto a mandrel. The glass must be heated slowly to the right temperature. Some glass even changes colors permanently when heated. To prevent sticking, coat the mandrel with a special bead release prior to use. As the molten glass passes to the mandrel, turn the rod in the flame to help to make the bead smooth and round, hence the name: "wound work." Glass rods are available in many strengths, colors, patterns, opacities and melting points. The viscosity of the glass is also an important factor. If you plan to mix glasses, be sure they are compatible.

Suppliers often sell sample kits so you can try out different types of glass. Knowing the properties of the glass is essential.

Beads can be encased in a layer of clear glass, which will magnify and add depth to the bead. To change the shape of the bead, use a series of graphite paddles. Add effects to your bead with other materials compatible with glass, such as powders, enamels and foils. Add glass designs, like raised dots, lines or squiggles, from a glass stringer.

• *Moretti or Effetre is a medium-soft Italian glass popular with beadmakers and available in many colors. Most beginners start with Moretti glass.*

• *Bullseye is slightly harder glass made in Portland, Ore., and available in an array of opalescent and transparent colors.*

• *Borosilicate glass is a hard, dense glass that passes from fluid to solid rather quickly at high temperatures. Beadmakers love it for its clarity, durability and unusual effects.*

• *Dichroic literally means "two-colored." Dichroic glass is impregnated with metal oxides that give it a rich, iridescent quality.*

• *Satake is a soft glass from Japan that is hand pulled and available in a unique range of colors.*

• *Lauscha is a medium-soft German glass especially created for glass flame work. The use of different types of glass will help you create desired shapes, sizes, colors and textures.*

*Michelle McKenzie Lampwork and Design: Jungle Bracelet.*

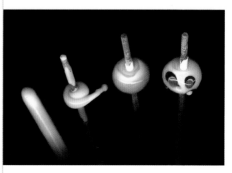

**Art and Soul of Glass Beads**, Creating Lampwork by Tamara Knight. Photographer Richard Pearce.

*Tamara Knight: Water and Beach Pebbles Bracelet.*

Once the bead cools, clean the bead release from the hole of the bead and remove any burrs. Examine your bead for imperfections or cracks. If you were successful, the bead will be ready to string.

Several companies make interchangeable bead pendants for showing off beads from your lampwork collection. Look in recent issues of bead magazines and bead catalogs to find the one you like the best.

*Susan Ray: Clear Waters Lampwork Necklace with Metal Clay Silver Pendant. Lampwork by Bob Leonardo.*

When a bead's hole is too large for your flexible wire, insert seed beads or a bugle bead to hold the bead in place.

*Lampwork by Michelle McKenzie: Jelly Bead. Courtesy of McKenzie Glassworks.*

A focal bead — or several focal beads — draws the eye to areas of interest. Beads that accent focal beads are sometimes called "adjacent" or "secondary" beads. The adjacent beads should not distract from the focal beads. Instead, they should reinforce the characteristics of the focal beads and complement their colors, shapes and textures.

*"Melting glass in the flame can become a lifetime passion."*

— Karen Leonardo

*Karen Leonardo: Golden Scepter beads/ Ancient series.*

Although there are many magazines and books about creating lampwork, you may want to take a class at your local university, glass center or art center — or private classes available from a local glass artist. Today, classes are fairly easy to find.

# CHAPTER SIX

# STRINGING
# BASICS

# STRINGING

*With Sue Wilke and Susan Ray*

Stringing is basic. Remember the days when you made necklaces from macaroni shells? The principle is the same. Today you will use better materials and learn to finish your piece using a different method than tying a knot, but all in all, not much has changed since those early days. You will feel the same excitement as you did when you first strung those macaroni shells.

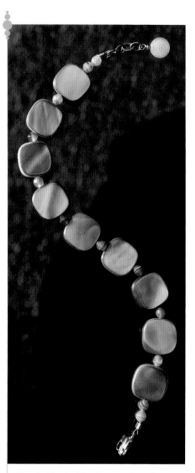

*Sherrie Chapin: Autumn Coin Bracelet.*
*Courtesy of Blue Moon.*

*Sherrie Chapin: Blue Between Bracelet.*
*Courtesy of Blue Moon.*

# Single-Strand Basics
## CRIMP BEADS

Use only precious-metal crimps. They hold up better. Sterling silver crimps are more flexible and respond easily to flattening. Base metal crimps sometimes can crack and wear, leaving you to pick up handfuls of beads. Make sure the package says sterling. The word silver may only represent the base metal color. Also, if the crimps are too soft, the wire eventually will work its way loose. Use a reputable brand of sterling silver crimps. (See Rio Grande, Resource Guide, page 214.)

What size crimp beads do you need? Crimp bead sizes, material and color are a personal preference, but 2mm x 3mm sterling silver crimps last the best for up to medium-weight pieces and they won't loosen after months (or years) of wear.

*NOTE:* Try to add a sterling- or gold-plate 2mm or 3mm ball to the end of your stringing right before your crimp bead. The additional ball helps to reduce the wear and tear each crimp bead takes. String the flexible wire back through the crimp bead and ball and at least 1" of beads before cutting away the short end.

If you are stringing heavy glass or natural beads, you can insert crimp beads every 3" or 4". Crimp as you go. Such crimps add much-needed security so your piece will stay crimped. Crimps can be hidden inside beads or spacers.

## FLEXIBLE WIRE

Flexible wire today comes in a large variety of colors, strands, strengths and sizes. See Fire Mountain Gems or Rio Grande in the Resource Guide for more information, page 214. Flexible wires can stretch, especially when your necklace contains heavier beads, so it is important to choose the right diameter of wire and be conscious of the weight of your beads when selecting flexible wire for your piece. Be sure to keep your jewelry flat (not hung) in a clean, dry area. Use the best flexible wire you can find. Many brands are strong and pliable. Read the manufacturer's recommendations before use.

Beginners should try seven-strand .019 diameter silver-gray for starters. This is also called "craft wire" in your local craft stores.

### HOW TO CHOOSE WIRE

*.014 diameter wire is best for small projects, seed beads, lightweight crystals and pearls. It is very flexible. See Purple Passions Pearl Necklace, page 29.*

*.019 diameter wire is the most common choice. It works best with medium-weight beads of all types and assures strength and durability for most projects. This diameter is used most often in this book. See Chicago Sunrise Pendant Necklace, page 139.*

*.024 diameter wire, generally the "heavyweight," is considered best when you are working with heavy beads, such as lampwork, large gemstones or pendants, or ceramic beads. It is very strong. It can also be used for beading that will need to absorb a lot of movement, such as watches, bracelets, eyeglass holders or lariats. I also like to use this diameter of wire when I use many, or especially large, polymer beads.*

*See Red Flame Necklace, page 33.*

*Some vendors also have lighter weights of wire, such as .010 diameter, that are designed for knitting or crocheting. See Bead Crochet, page 154.*

And, as with all things, enjoy what you are doing. If your budget requires you to find beads that cost less than $10, don't fret. This won't diminish the enjoyment of making your bracelet or the excitement of seeing your creativity soar. It is the doing that really matters and the giving that is such a joy.

## FIT MATTERS

It is easy to start working with beads by making a bracelet. Most women have wrist sizes from 6½" to 8". If you are making a bracelet for yourself, simply try one on for size! Use another bracelet from your jewelry case as your guide. If you are unsure of the size for a friend, use a 7" length of the beads as a starting point and adjust this to the overall size of the wearer.

Consider the size of the beads in your design. When working with extra-large beads, compensate for their size by adding some length. It is best to size the bracelet on the wearer before adding the clasp.

*Remember:* If it doesn't fit, you can cut the wire (with wire cutters). Carefully slide the beads one at a time back onto the bead board in proper order and restring the piece. The second stringing will take little time, and this time the bracelet will have the proper fit.

Another method of changing the size of a bracelet is to add an extender. An extender is usually made up of a small piece of chain or beaded flexible wire between 2" and 6". The extender has an additional set of closures, so it will easily attach to other finished jewelry.

The instructions for making a single-strand bracelet or single-strand necklace are the same. Only the length of wire and number of beads are different, so once you learn these basic steps you can begin to make matching pieces.

# Basic Supplies

**Assorted beads:** Gather 20 to 30 beads for a bracelet and 60 or more beads for a necklace, depending on their shape (with an average size of 6mm).

**Bead board:** Use one that will comfortably meet the needs of the size of your design, as well as your available work space.

**Containers:** Use a divided storage container or muffin tin or small jars for sorting beads.

**Flexible Wire:** A good basic wire is .019-gauge silver-gray flexible wire. A good rule of thumb for length is 12" for a standard single-strand bracelet and 1 yard for the longest of necklaces, lariats or eyeglass holders. For a 16"-18" necklace and a bracelet set, plan on using 1 yard. It is better to err on the side of more wire than less. Crimping an end that is short on wire can get pretty labor-intensive. So, in this instance, more is better.

**Split ring or jump ring (optional):** Use one in base metal: silver or gold. Split rings are more durable than jump rings.

**Crimp beads:** Use two 2mm x 3mm sterling silver, gold or vermeil crimp beads made of precious metals, not base metal.

**Seamless, round beads (optional):** Use two sterling silver, gold or vermeil 2mm to 3mm seamless, round beads to finish your bracelets and necklaces. Place them at each end of your project, just before the crimp bead, to help the crimp bead withstand some of the pressure placed on it during wear.

**Clasp:** Use a toggle set or lobster-claw clasp with a tab end in gold, silver, base metal, pewter or vermeil. If the tab end is not available, use a jump ring or a split ring instead.

# Single-Strand Bracelet Step-by-Step

Making a simple one-strand bracelet with a flexible wire and toggle clasp closure is a good way to begin beadwork.

The average time to complete a simple bracelet will be approximately 30 to 60 minutes.

*Be sure to avoid using beads that are too large near the sides of your wrist. As with necklaces, consider where on the wrist each bead will sit.*

## Choose Your Design

*With Sue Wilke*

There are unlimited patterns you can use to make a simple bracelet.

**Repeat pattern:** Use a simple line of beads in a specific pattern running from one end of the bracelet to the other. There are many combinations you can create by repeating bead arrangements.

**Centered:** Start with the center bead and work each side from the center outward. You can complete one side first and then match to the other side of the center bead.

**Bead filler:** Use seed bead combinations to fill in between focal beads — something I'm fond of doing. They add color without weight.

**Random:** Pile a handful of beads onto your bead board, then into the channel in the order they appear. Or, place an assortment of beads in your honey pot and string them in random order.

# Find Your Fit

To determine the size of your fin-ished bracelet, measure your wrist with a tape measure. You will need to add length to compensate for your closure. Your toggle clasp will add ½" to 1" to your finished work in most instances. If your wrist size is more than 6½", add beads to your bracelet. If your wrist size is smaller, use fewer beads.

## Test Your Design

Add a seed bead to one end of the cut wire and tie a knot. This is called a "stop" bead or "tension" bead and will prevent your stringing from falling off the end while you test your design.

Or, another simple method is to use a hemostat or other clamp.

## Add the Clasp

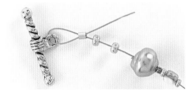

**Step B:** Hold the crimp bead in place and loop the end of flexible wire back through the crimp bead. Allow 1" of wire to pass through the crimp bead.

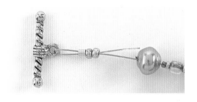

**Step C:** String the end through the first two or three beads on the strand.

**Step A:** When you are ready to add the first portion of the clasp to one end, string on the crimp bead, and allow it to slide 2" from the end. Then string on one end of the clasp.

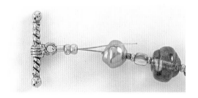

**Step D:** Pull the crimp beads up tight to the clasp.

**Step F:** Use a wire cutter to clip the excess from the shorter wire end and discard the clipped piece.

*If you miscut your short "tail" wire, simply separate the last bead away from the others and clip the short wire again. Then, slide the bead back into place and continue stringing. Those little wires, if not completely hidden inside a bead, can be quite an irritant to your skin during wear, so it's best to be sure they are properly cut.*

**Step E:** With flat-nose pliers, cover the crimp bead entirely, and press down firmly to flatten the crimp bead. Spin the crimp bead around, and press down firmly again. Your crimp bead should be uniformly flattened on both sides. Test the closure by pulling firmly on the wire to be sure the crimp bead will hold.

**Step G:** If desired, add a jump ring or split ring to the end of the toggle or lobster claw. Make sure the diameter of the additional split ring is small enough to fit through the toggle ring; otherwise you will be unable to close it once it is on your wrist. We use the half rule. The jump ring diameter must be less than half the size of the toggle's inside diameter.

# String Your Beads

**Step A:** String on your beads as desired. The first few beads on either end of your bracelet must have large-enough holes to accommodate both strands of wire. Avoid ending or starting with seed beads. These beads must be small enough to easily fit through a toggle closure. Try using 6/0 or 8/0 beads for ending, if possible. As you go, check to be sure that your short wire has remained strung within the first few beads and that no beads are "hung up" on the wire.

**Step B:** Finish the strand as you began, with the crimp bead and other side of your clasp, but check your fit before crimping.

# Check the Fit

If this is your first bracelet, try it on before completing it. Hold the open end firmly, or ask someone else to hold it for you, and wrap the bracelet around your wrist to see if your measurements were accurate. This is still a "trial-and-error" technique. Everyone has an imaginary point on his or her wrist that feels right, so it is best to have the wearer try on a few bracelets before making one for a friend.

# Add the Ending Clasp

**Step A:** Loop the end of the wire back through the crimp and two additional beads.

**Step B:** Snug the crimp and two end beads close to the toggle, pulling on the end to tighten any gaps of wire in the design. Be sure to string through the clasp, crimp and several beads all at once.

**Step C:** Once the short wire has been pulled as far as possible, hold the bracelet vertically with the finished end down, and make sure no space remains between any of the beads. Sometimes a bead will get "hung up" on the wire, and more often than not, it won't be discovered until after you have flattened your second crimp bead. Take the time now to inspect your work. Again, check for proper fit on your wrist before crimping.

**Step D:** Flatten the crimp and cut the wire, just as in Steps E and F on page 117.

> **EASY DOES IT...**
>
> It is easiest to pull the wire through the crimp and end beads if you can keep the crimp bead away from the clasp end as you go. Slide the crimp bead as close to the beads as you can while you feed the wire through. Sometimes, if enough wire remains, you can simply feed the loop until most of the wire has been strung in place. Other times, you will need the aid of the flat-nose pliers to hold the short end of the wire and pull it taut.

# Attach an Extender Chain

*Sherrie Chapin. Courtesy of Blue Moon.*

> Work from the clasp end to the chain.
> Adding the chain last, you can make it
> any finished length.

**Step A:** String a crimp bead, and
then the extender chain on the end,
bringing the same end of the wire
back through the crimp bead.

**Step B:** Slide the crimp bead up to the
chain, allowing the rest of wire through
crimp. Crimp using crimping pliers.
Tuck in ½" of wire through the beads
and cut the rest with cutters.

# Growing Your Design From Bracelet to Necklace

Extending your beaded bracelet to create a necklace design is easy.

**Step A:** Lay your bracelet in the second channel of your bead tray.

**Step B:** Find and sort beads that are the same as or similar to the bracelet beads.

**Step C:** Duplicate the bracelet design by repeating the chosen beads, placing them into the first channel of the bead tray.

**Step D:** Make some decisions about the design. Is the necklace long enough? Do you want to continue the same pattern?

**Step E:** If you decide to continue the same pattern, move your bracelet to the left or right of the beads, and continue to copy the pattern until you have reached the desired length.

**Step F:** Do you want to alter the pattern? Start with the same beads that you used to duplicate the bracelet. Alter them on either side of the newly created portion of the necklace. You will be able to play with the arrangement until you are comfortable with your new design.

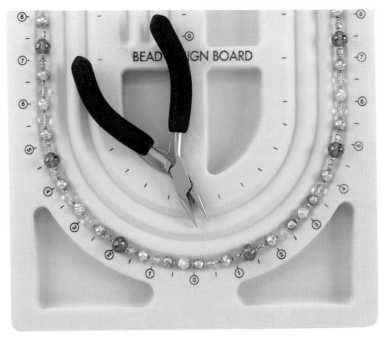

*Whether you are continuing the pattern of the bracelet for your necklace or making a whole new look, laying the work onto the first channel of the bead board allows you to play with the different options before stringing.*

**Step G:** Consider whether the necklace will be under a shirt collar, where it could become uncomfortable if the beads are too large and higher up on the neckline. Graduating the size of the beads to smaller and smaller ones as they reach the back of the neck is a good solution.

**Step H:** Experiment. Add beads that were not used in the original bracelet. Move aside some of the duplicated design and insert the new additions. Continue to add the new beads as the necklace evolves.

# Single-Strand Necklace Basics

To make a single-strand necklace, follow the same steps for a single-strand bracelet. The only differences are the length of the finished piece and number of beads.

**Step A:** Determine the size of your finished necklace.

**Step B:** If you are making a choker, measure your neck with a string at the position you want the necklace to rest.

**Step C:** Add 1" to your neck measurement for the correct size of your finished piece.

**Step D:** Add 4" to the desired finished necklace length to determine the length of wire to cut.

*If your beads are exceptionally large, you may need to add more length to compensate for the additional diameter of the large beads. Plan for more wire accordingly.*

# Multi-Strand Basics

*With Sue Wilke*

*Susan Ray: Salon Multi-Strand Necklace.*

> *Multi-strands use the same technique as single-strands. You are just adding more strands to your closure loop (or split ring).*

**Same length:** The strands may be the same length, but they will need to be slightly longer than a single strand by itself, because the multi-strands take more room to sit together on top of the wrist or neck. Also, more slack is taken up by all the strands coming together at the clasp.

**Torsade:** The strands are all of equal length and before you hook the clasp to wear it, you twist the strand several times. This can be an elegant look, but it does take quite a bit more length to allow for the twists.

**Graduated:** One strand can be slightly smaller in length than the next so the strands sit one on top of the other. This is a flattering look in any length necklace. The graduated strand technique is easy to achieve with a multi-channel bead board. The outside channel, or the one closest to the edge of the board, is the longest and the most accurate for length. By creating additional strands in other channels and ending them at the same point, you are actually creating a graduated multi-strand design.

*Wendy Mullane: Ocean Sands Bracelet.*

# Making a Multi-Strand Bracelet

To complete a multi-strand bracelet with equal-length strands, repeat the instructions in the Single-Strand Bracelet Step-by-Step, pages 113 to 120, for each strand of the bracelet. Complete one strand at a time. The only difference: Add 1" to your measured wrist length.

Also, when you lay out your patterns of beads on the multi-channel bead board, alternate large and small beads on each strand so the prominence of focal beads will be enhanced and larger beads won't collide.

*When making multi-strand bracelets, keep the clasp loop with each consecutive wire strand in the same order on each side.*

Use the how-to photos here for additional guidance, if necessary, as you finish the second strand.

## FINISH THE ADDITIONAL STRANDS

**Step A:** Use hemostats or bead stoppers to hold the end of the second beaded strand.

**Step B:** Finish the strand with small beads and the crimp bead.

**Step C:** Loop the wire through the clasp, then back through the crimp and first two beads on the strand, just as you did with the first strand.

**Step D:** Finish by pulling the crimp snug to the clasp. Check the length around your wrist, then flatten the crimp bead on both sides. Snip the excess wire tail.

# Multi-Strand Necklace

To complete a multi-strand necklace or choker, follow the multi-strand bracelet instructions. First decide what style of necklace you'd like (same length, graduated strands or torsade) and cut each wire strand accordingly. A multi-channel bead board will help you determine the number of beads in each strand. Be generous with your wire so you won't be disappointed. Once you have decided on the finished length for your necklace, add at least 4" to that amount to determine what length to cut the wire.

*Don't flatten the final crimp on each strand until you are finished with all of the strands. This gives you one last chance to alter your designs. Avoid tugging on the strands while checking their length, as the unflattened crimp could come loose. When you are finished stringing, check that each wire is taut, and flatten the crimps.*

*Eileen Feldman: Heart's Delight Necklace.*

# CHAPTER SEVEN

## FINDINGS AND CLOSURES

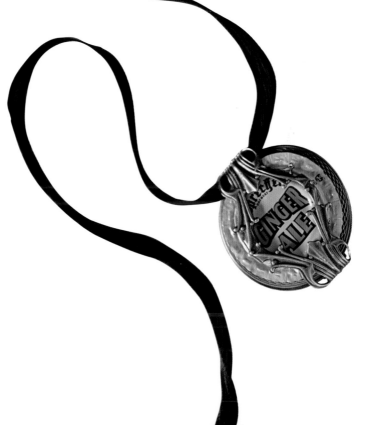

# FINDINGS

| | | | | |
|---|---|---|---|---|
| Bell Caps | Crimps | Eye Pin | Eyeglass Holder | French Hook - A |
| French Hook - B | French Hook - C | Head Pin Style Earring | Head Pin | Hook & Clasp |
| Jump Rings | Split Rings | Kidney Earwires | Lever Back 1 | Lever Back 2 |
| Lobster Claws | Metal Spacers | Rondelle | Snap on Pendant Bail | Spring Clasp |
| Spring Rings | Tab End | Toggle Clasp 1 | Toggle Clasp 2 | "S" Clasp |

Jewelry findings are available at craft and specialty bead stores and in mail order catalogs. With some luck, you can find wonderful vintage findings at thrift and resale shops.

Other types of findings and closures are almost infinite, from base metals to precious metals and reclaimed antique clasps to contemporary toggles and everything in between. You will find something perfect for every project. See Resource Guide, pages 214.

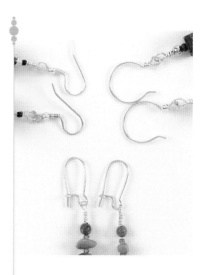

## Ear Wires

Ear wires are available in many styles. Try on ear wires before buying too many. Different styles of ear wires fit the ear differently. Surgical steel and sterling are best for sensitive ears.

## Crimps

A cardinal rule: "Don't skimp on crimps." Crimps are available in many weights and materials. Use crimp beads that are at least half-hard silver and a heavy-gauge wire. Available from bead stores and bead distributors, these crimps are more expensive, but worth every penny. Quality crimps ensure you will enjoy your new beaded jewelry for

*Barbara Markoe: Confetti Earrings.*

years to come. You can use 2 x 3mm and 2 x 2mm half-hard sterling silver crimps in heavier-gauge wire for the majority of your work.

## Clasps

When choosing a necklace clasp, be sure it is appropriate for the piece's weight or number of strands. Also, consider how it will feel on the back of your neck.

Clasps are available in many new styles. If you prefer toggles, be sure that the bar end is larger than the loop end. This will help ensure that the toggle stays in place when you wear your jewelry. Make sure the first few beads nearest the bar end will slip easily through the loop end, or you won't be able to use the toggle closure without a struggle.

Lobster claws and/or toggle clasps can add interest when placed to one side of your design, such as the front bottom. This also makes it easier for older fingers to clasp.

## TOGGLE CLASP STEP-BY-STEP

Toggles seem to be a favorite style to use for bracelets. A toggle clasp is easy to fasten with one hand when putting on jewelry by yourself. .

**Step A:** Toggle clasps can be tricky to use when creating multiple strands. Be sure that the bar end of the toggle can fit easily through the ring with the beads on the strand. Beads that are too large near the bar end may prevent the bar from threading through the loop end.

**Step B:** Cut your wire with some additional length, then string your beads and add the crimp beads, but do not crimp. The extra length will help secure the beads while you try on the piece.

**Step C:** Once you are sure you can easily thread the bar end through the loop, complete the crimping.

**Step D:** Thread the short end of wire through several beads and crimp. Trim away the excess wire.

## BUTTON LOOP CLOSURE STEP-BY-STEP

An interesting, inexpensive closure can be made from a shank button and a beaded loop. Here's how to start stringing your piece for a button loop closure:

**Step A:** Cut the desired length of wire, and thread a crimp bead onto it.

**Step B:** Thread on an odd number of seed beads. The length that the seed beads cover the wire should equal ¼"

more in length than the diameter of the button. This will allow the button to slide through the loop.

**Step C:** After you have threaded the appropriate number of seed beads, thread your wire back through the crimp.

**Step D:** Pull on both wires together as you push the crimp toward the loop of seed beads to remove any slack.

**Step E:** Flatten the crimp.

*The finished loop.*

**Step F:** String your strand as usual, covering your tail of wire next to the crimp with two or three beads.

*The finished button end.*

**Step G:** On the other end of the string, attach the button as you would any other clasp.

*Jeanne Holland: Lion Serpent Lariat.*

**Step A:** If you are using flexible wire, place a small seed bead on the end, after your crimp. The seed bead will act as the "stop" bead.

**Step B:** Loop your wire around the seed bead and back through the crimp bead. Pull the wire taut.

**Step C:** Crimp down, and voila — a lariat. No clasp needed!

## Spacers

Spacers often refer to metal beads that separate other beads in your design, although spacers can be made of other materials as well. Spacer beads are available in a variety of metals: silver, bronze, pewter, gold and other base metals. To get an antique look, vendors add a patina to the metal, which highlights intricate details. To lessen the expense, you can use base-metal spacers colored to resemble silver, pewter and gold. Craft stores, as well as specialty bead stores, have a large, inexpensive assortment.

## Lariats

There is no closure easier than no clasp at all. A lariat design loops through itself, or the two ends can be gently tied together in an overhand knot, which allows the ends or tassels to hang free.

# Found Objects

*With Jessica Italia*

When planning to use found objects in your jewelry designs, check for burrs or sharp edges before beginning to work with the pieces. Spray them with clear acrylic Rust-Oleum or paint with clear nail polish. This will prevent rust from getting on your clothing when the pieces are worn.

*Jessica Italia: Rock Star Weekend Earrings. Courtesy of Galena Beads.*

*Jessica Italia: She Who Holds the Key. Courtesy of Galena Beads.*

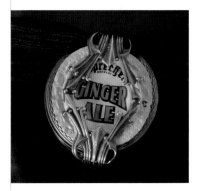

*Jessica Italia: Soda Pop Crush Necklace. Courtesy of Galena Beads.*

# Vintage Findings

*With Wendy Mullane and Jeanne
Holland of Vintaj Natural Brass Co.*

*Jeanne Holland: Art Deco Revival Necklace.*

*Wendy Mullane: Earthen Elements Bracelet.*

What a privilege it is to live in the
midst of such an extraordinary,
eclectic design movement. This is an
era when the evolution of jewelry
design throughout the ages is here to
draw on for inspiration. You have, at
your fingertips, the new technologies
of today combined with the natural
and artisan materials of yesterday.
Vintaj Natural Brass, a timeless metal,
is inspired by earlier generations. It
takes us into the future, combining
old-world and contemporary techniques. Imagine the possibilities!

Design in the era of your choosing: art
nouveau, Art and Crafts, Victorian or
contemporary. Whatever the era, your
design will be bolstered by the rich
quality of these metals.

As you look at your completed design,
don't blink to see more clearly. Your eyes
aren't playing tricks on you — it really
does look genuinely engraved in the
era you've designed it after. This is due

to the inherent quality of natural brass. Vintaj findings are 100 percent natural brass. They are not antique-plated or chemically treated and they are nickel-free. One of their unique characteristics is their rich caramel color, which is identical to vintage brass. Superior design and workmanship went into the original vintage tooling used to strike many of these findings. They wear gracefully through time and become keepsakes.

So, grab a handful of findings and beads and take off on your journey through time. You may even find yourself drifting into design land in the catacombs of Egypt, or in Monet's garden. Wherever your inspiration, Vintaj Brass will take you there.

> *Vintaj original art jewelry is designed using an innovative "brass-encased glass" settings concept developed by Wendy Mullane and Jeanne Holland. (See project designs on pages 136, 148 and 159.)*

## Jump Rings

Jump rings are small but versatile connectors used for jewelry projects of all kinds. The more you practice working with jump rings, the better you will get.

When opening a jump ring, take care not to lose the tension of the circle. The best way to open a jump ring is to use two pairs of pliers, one in each hand, as follows:

**Step A:** With the circle facing you, gently grasp each side of the jump ring next to the opening.

**Step B:** Push one side of the jump ring away from you while pulling the other one toward you. This side-to-side motion keeps the integrity of the circular shape. Extending the ends away from each other would distort the ring.

**Step C:** Slide the open ring through the attachments or connections.

**Step D:** Push the ends of the jump ring back to the center to close it.

When you are using a jump ring, be sure to check that it is completely closed. Even the smallest opening will allow attachments to come loose. When using precious metals, many jewelers will solder jump rings closed.

*Jessica Italia: Playin' In Ma's Button Jar Bracelet.*

**FIX A BROKEN CLASP**

*Broken clasp? You may not need to restring it. Simply place a split ring or jump ring through the loop at the end of the flexible wire next to the crimp. Then you can safely cut away the broken clasp. Secure the new clasp to the split ring.*

# CREATE YOUR OWN JUMP RINGS

**Step A:**

Coil a length of 18- to 22-gauge wire around a mandrel by hand or by using other wire-coiling tools available in craft stores, online or through specialty bead shops.

**Step B:**

Use wire cutters to cut a complete link from the coil.

**Step C:**

Close each link tightly when connecting them together or to other portions of a piece you are working on.

Check to see that the gauge of the jump ring is heavy enough to secure attachments.

# THREE-WAY CONNECTORS

*Deanna Killackey: Chicago Sunrise Necklace.*

## MAKING A DOUBLE-LOOPED PENDANT

This technique will allow you to hang a dangle from a pendant while stringing the pendant on the necklace from behind the bead.

### Tools to Have on Hand

Wire cutter
Round-nose pliers

### Gathering Your Goods

Small glass bead
2 seed beads
Medium-size pendant with holes in back
Large-size pendant
Headpin
Eyepin

### TASK 1: STRINGING BEADS

**Step A:** String a glass bead and two seed beads onto a headpin. Using round-nose pliers, make a basic loop on top of the wire. Set the pendant aside.

**Step B:** Next, string the larger pendant (in this case it is a flower with vertical holes on the back of the bead) on an eyepin. Use round-nose pliers to create a basic loop.

### TASK 2: CONNECTING THE PENDANTS

**Step A:** Gently open the eyepin. Affix the smaller pendant to the larger one.

**Step B:** String the larger pendant onto a necklace.

# MANDALA CIRCLE BRACELET

*With Barbara Markoe*

*Barbara Markoe: Mandala Bracelet.*
*Photography by Barbara Markoe.*
*Lampwork by Bob Leonardo.*

**Finished Size:** Adjustable, 6½" to 8"

**Expense:** Less than $25

**Expertise:** Beginner/intermediate

**Time to Complete:** An evening

## Gathering Your Goods

Silver or semi-precious beads, 2mm to 5mm or even tiny seed beads

7 Jump rings, 10mm

3 Lampwork beads

Jewelry glue

Focal bead

10 lb. test fishing line (Buy a whole spool at a sporting goods store. It will last a lifetime.)

1 spool each of 16-gauge and 24-gauge wire

**Where to Find:** Specialty bead stores, catalog suppliers, artisans

## Tools to Have on Hand

Flush wire cutter

Wire cutter

Round-nose pliers

Chain-nose pliers

Chasing hammer

Bench block or anvil

## CREATING THE BEAD CIRCLE
### TASK 1: PREPPING THE LINE

**Step A:** Clip a small piece of fishing line. The length depends on the size of the circle you want, but generally 8" is sufficient. Remember, fishing line is cheap, so use 2' feet if you're more comfortable!

**Step B:** Tie a loose knot on one end of the fishing line, leaving about an inch. This is only so your beads won't fall off as you string.

### TASK 2: STRINGING

**Step A:** Start stringing your beads. They can be all the same or a variety. About 12 of the 4mm to 5mm beads make a nice size circle.

**Step B:** Keep stringing until you have the size you are happy with.

### TASK 3: FINISHING THE CIRCLE

**Step A:** Gently untie the knot in the end. If you're not holding both ends, your beads will fall off.

**Step B:** With both ends, tie a knot just as you would if you were tying a package. Be sure to knot twice, and make sure it's tight.

**Step C:** Add a drop of glue to the center of the knot for holding power. Let it dry for a few minutes.

**Step D:** When the glue is dry snip the ends of the fishing line close to the knot.

> *Before tying off, link each consecutive ring with the one before it.*

## BUILDING THE BRACELET
### TASK 1: ADDING LAMPWORK COMPONENTS

**Step A:** Cut a 3" piece of 16-gauge wire.

**Step B:** Make an eye loop in one end.

**Step C:** With your chasing hammer and anvil or bench block, gently hammer the eye to give it a flattened look. Remember: It's tap, tap, tap — not pound, pound, pound.

**Step D:** Add a lampwork bead.

**Step E:** Clip the remaining wire to the approximate length to make an eye loop on the opposite end of the bead. This is Lampwork component 1

**Step F:** Repeat these steps for the remaining lampwork beads.

### TASK 2: ATTACHING JUMP RINGS

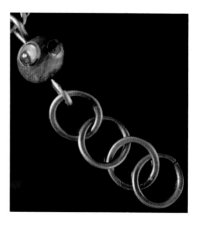

**Step A:** Use your chasing hammer to gently tap until the jump rings have a flattened appearance.

**Step B:** Attach four jump rings together, and attach the end jump ring to Lampwork component 1.

**Step C:** Attach the twisted jump ring to Lampwork component 1 and 2.

**Step D:** Attach a jump ring to Lampwork component 2 and to the beaded circle.

**Step E:** Attach the beaded circle to the square focal bead.

## TASK 3: WRAPPING THE JUMP RING

**Step A:** Using your 24-gauge wire, wrap the jump ring that connects the focal bead and Lampwork component 3.

**Step B:** When finished, clip both ends and crimp to jump ring. Adjust coils.

## TASK 4: ADDING THE CLASP

**Step A:** Flatten one end of the 2" 16-gauge wire with your chasing hammer and bench block.

**Step B:** With the tip of the chain-nose pliers, create a small loop at the end where the wire is flat.

**Step C:** In the back or largest part of the round-nose pliers, form a loop in the opposite direction of the small loop you made previously.

**Step D:** On the other end of your 2" wire, make a small eye. This will attach to the eye loop from Lampwork component 3.

**Step E:** Use your chasing hammer and bench block to flatten the hook and eye. Attach them to your bracelet.

# MIXED METALS NECKLACE

*With Jenni Moore*

*Jenni Moore: Mixed Metals Necklace. Courtesy of Beadazzled*

**Designer:** Jenni Moore

**Finished Size:** 19½" including cones, but not clasp

**Expense:** $25 to $50

**Expertise:** Intermediate

**Time to Complete:** A day

## Tools to Have on Hand

Round-nose pliers

Chain-nose pliers

Wire cutter

Crimping pliers

Bead Stoppers (or use a hemostat)

**Where to Find:** Specialty bead stores

## Gathering Your Goods

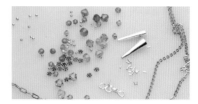

*Courtesy of Beadazzled. Photography by Cas Webber.*

**A:** 6 padparadscha 6mm Swarovski crystal bicones

**B:** 6 Light Colorado topaz 6mm Swarovski crystal bicones

**C:** 6 lime 6mm Swarovski crystal bicones

**D:** 6 topaz 6mm Swarovski crystal bicones

**E:** 13 padparadscha 4mm Swarovski crystal bicones

**F:** 13 Light Colorado topaz 4mm Swarovski crystal bicones

**G:** 13 lime 4mm Swarovski crystal bicones

**H:** 13 topaz 4mm Swarovski crystal bicones

**I:** 48 Indian silver 4mm daisy spacers

**J:** 104 sterling silver 2mm smooth round beads

5 g sterling silver 4 mm tube beads

19" gold-filled drawn cable chain

19" copper cable chain

3 yds. fine (.014) beading wire – cut into three equal pieces

6 sterling silver 2 x 2mm crimp beads

2 Southwestern style sterling silver cones

1' sterling silver 22-gauge dead-soft wire

Sterling silver hook clasp

## TASK 1: SETTING UP

**Step A:** Cut two 6" pieces of 22-gauge wire. Set one aside.

**Step B:** Use your round-nose pliers to create a loop about halfway down the remaining piece of wire.

*Courtesy of Beadazzled. Photography by Cas Webber.*

**Step C:** Hook the end links of both your gold-filled and copper cable chains into the loop you just created.

*Courtesy of Beadazzled. Photography by Cas Webber.*

**Step D:** Close off the loop. Remember that you already made the first loop

**Step E:** Attach the three pieces of beading wire to the loop. Crimp the wire.

## TASK 2: STRINGING STRAND 1

**Step A:** Using one of the pieces of beading wire you just crimped, string on four silver tube beads.

**Step B:** String accent beads in clusters of three (a silver bead, a crystal, and a silver bead) with three silver tube beads between each cluster. String the accent clusters. (Remember the silver tube beads between each bead cluster!):

**J-G-J; J-H-J; I-B-I; J-E-J; J-G-J; I-D-I; J-F-J; J-E-J; I-C-I; J-H-J; J-F-J; I-A-I; J-G-J; J-H-J; I-B-I; J-E-J; J-G-J; I-D-I; J-F-J; J-E-J; I-C-I; J-H-J; J-F-J; I-A-I; J-G-J; J-H-J**

**Step C:** Immediately after the last J bead, finish off the strand with four silver tube beads.

**Step D:** Secure the loose end of the beading wire in a bead stopper.

## TASK 3: STRINGING STRAND 2

**Step A:** Using the second piece of beading wire you crimped onto your loop, string three silver tube beads.

**Step B:** String the accent clusters for the second strand in the following order. Remember to string three silver tube beads between each cluster:

**J-F-J; I-A-I; J-G-J; J-H-J; I-B-I; J-E-J; J-G-J; I-D-I; J-F-J; J-E-J; I-C-I; J-H-J; J-F-J; I-A-I; J-G-J; J-H-J; I-B-I; J-E-J; J-G-J; I-D-I; J-F-J; J-E-J; I-C-I; J-H-J; J-F-J; J-E-J**

**Step C:** Immediately after the last J bead, finish off the strand with three silver tube beads.

**Step D:** Secure the loose end of the beading wire in a bead stopper.

## TASK 4: STRINGING STRAND 3

**Step A:** Using the final piece of beading wire you crimped onto your loop, string five silver tube beads.

**Step B:** String the accent clusters for the third strand in the following order. Remember to string three silver tube beads between each cluster:

**J-G-J; I-A-I; J-F-J; J-H-J; I-C-I; J-E-J; J-F-J; I-D-I; J-G-J; J-E-J; I-B-I; J-H-J; J-G-J; I-A-I; J-F-J; J-H-J; I-C-I; J-E-J; J-F-J; I-D-I; J-G-J; J-E-J; I-B-I; J-H-J**

**Step C:** Immediately after the last J bead, finish off the strand with five silver tube beads.

**Step D:** Secure the loose end of the beading wire with a bead stopper.

## TASK 5: ADDING A CONE

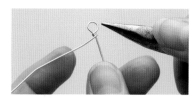

*Courtesy of Beadazzled. Photography by Cas Webber.*

**Step A:** Use your round-nose pliers to create a loop about halfway down the piece of wire. Hook the loose end of both pieces of chain into the loop as you did before.

**Step B:** Close off the loop using the simple wrapped loop method on page 145.

**Step C:** Remove the Bead Stopper and crimp the loose ends of the beading wire to the loop you just created.

***HINT:*** Your necklace will lay better if you attach the strands in the same order, from left to right, as they were attached on the first loop.

**Step D:** Attach the cones and clasp to your necklace.

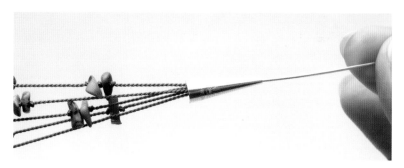

*Courtesy of Beadazzled. Photography by Cas Webber.*

# BEADED TOGGLE BAR AND RING CLASP

*With Wendy Mullane*

*Wendy Mullane: Mariner's Expedition Bracelet. Courtesy of Vintaj Natural Brass Co./ Galena Beads.*

**Designer:** Wendy Mullane

**Tools to Have on Hand**

Chain-nose pliers (2 pair)

**Gathering Your Goods**

3 natural brass 4mm melon spacer beads

2 aqua (Pacific opal) crystal bicones

2 natural brass 6mm flower spacers

2 brass eyepins, 1½"

8 natural brass 4mm jump rings

12 natural brass 4.5mm jump rings

2 natural brass ⅞" hammered ring drops

2 natural brass 8mm jump rings

**Where to Find:** Vintaj Natural Brass Co, Resource Guide, page 214

> *If you're looking for a simpler toggle bar, replace the hand-beaded toggle bar with a basic natural brass toggle bar. It will save time and money.*

## TASK 1: CONNECTING JUMP RINGS

**Step A:** Connect three 4.5mm jump rings together and set aside.

## TASK 2: ADDING BEADS AND RINGS

**Step A:** String the following onto the 1½" eyepin: one melon spacer bead, four 4mm jump rings, one aqua bicone, four 4.5mm jump rings, one flower spacer bead. Add the top ring of the three-ring section created in Task 1. Repeat the previous sequence in reverse. The three-ring section will become the toggle bar hanger.

**Step B:** Lay two hammered ring drops back to back. Attach a 4.5mm jump ring to the lined-up holes on the rings. Set aside.

**Step C:** Open one 8mm jump ring, and insert one flower spacer bead. Close the ring. Set aside.

**Step D:** Open a second 8mm jump ring. Slide on the hammered rings and the ringed flower spacer bead, and close.

*Wendy Mullane: Mariner's Expedition Bracelet.*

# BRACELET AND NECKLACE EXTENDERS

*With Sherrie Chapin*

Add length to a bracelet or necklace by attaching a piece of chain for an extender. You can create it with a split ring or jump ring. Optional: Add an additional lobster-claw clasp.

*Sherrie Chapin: Blue Between Bracelet. Courtesy of Blue Moon.*

## Gathering Your Goods

Sterling crimp beads
Flexible beading wire
Beads
Sterling chain
Lobster clasp
Sterling wire

## Tools to Have on Hand

Crimping pliers
Wire cutters
Flat-nose pliers

## TASK 1: ATTACHING THE CLASP AND CRIMP BEAD

*Courtesy of Sherrie Chapin, Blue Moon.*

**Step A:** String a crimp bead and then the lobster clasp on the flexible wire. Bring the same end of the wire back through the crimp bead.

**Step B:** Slide the crimp bead up to the clasp, allowing ½" wire through the crimp. Crimp it.

## TASK 2: STRINGING BEADS

**Step A:** String on your beads in the order desired.

## TASK 3: ATTACHING THE EXTENDER CHAIN AND CRIMP BEAD

*Courtesy of Sherrie Chapin, Blue Moon.*

**Step A:** String a crimp bead and then the extender chain on the end of your piece. Bring the same end of the wire back through the crimp bead.

**Step B:** Slide the crimp bead up to the chain, allowing the rest of the wire through the crimp.

**Step C:** Add an accent bead to the end of the extender chain. See Creating a Dangle.

**Note:** You can purchase commercially-made bracelet and necklace extenders from Rio Grande. See Resource Guide, page 214.

# CREATING A DANGLE

**Toolbox:**
Round-nose pliers
Wire cutters
Flat-nose pliers

### Gathering Your Goods
One 1½"-3" head pin
Desired beads

**Step A:** Add your bead(s) to your headpin. Stop 1" (or more) before the end of the pin.

**Step B:** Place your round-nose pliers ¼" from your last bead. Using your thumb and forefinger, bend the wire over the back of your pliers.

**Step C:** Cross the wire underneath and in front of the stationary wire, forming the start of a loop.

**Step D:** Complete the turn. Grasp the new loop with your round-nose pliers and turn it several times. When the turns get close to the bead(s), stop, and cut away the excess wire.

**Step E:** Use your flat-nose pliers to tuck in the cut end of the wire.

# CHAPTER EIGHT
## STITCHERY

# BASIC CROCHET

Basic crochet is easy. Many of us remember days at our grandmother's house learning to crochet potholders. A lot has changed since the days of crocheting with yarn. Today, wire crochet makes a fun jewelry project. Even the youngest enthusiast can learn this simple technique.

If you never have crocheted before, it might be best to learn to crochet using a skein of yarn rather than wire. Choose a yarn that is a medium weight, solid color and an acrylic-polyester blend. Avoid fancy yarns so you can concentrate on your technique. Pick a medium-size aluminum crochet hook (G-6) that is comfortable in your hands.

**Step A:** Start by making a simple slip knot with one end of your yarn from the skein. (For practice, you do not need to cut a piece of yarn from the skein.)

**Step B:** Slip the knot over the crochet hook, and tighten it.

**Step C:** Hold the crochet hook with your dominant hand.

**Step D:** Place the wire over the hook. Pinch the loop (from under the crochet hook) with the fingers of your non-dominant hand to help you easily pull the yarn through the knot on the hook.

**Step E:** Slip the knot over the crochet hook. This forms your first chain.

**Step F:** Pull to tighten up the new loop that remains on the hook.

**Step G:** Form another loop over your hook. Pass the wire through this loop already on your hook, allowing it to again slip from the hook to create your second chain. Pull the wire to tighten it. Each loop that slips from the hook forms a stitch in a basic crochet chain.

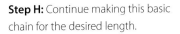

**Step H:** Continue making this basic chain for the desired length.

**Step I:** To create a continuous circle: insert your hook through the first stitch in the chain. (Each chain stitch is made of three loops, two on the top and one loop on the bottom. Insert your hook under the top two loops of the stitch). Pass the wire through both the loop already on your hook and this first stitch, allowing loops to slip off the hook. Tighten your new loop. Now the ends of your chain are joined to form a circle. (Be sure you check your chain for twists before you join it.)

**Step J:** To begin a slipstitch necklace, continue to insert the hook through the top two loops in the chain, one at a time. Pull the wire through both the loop already on your hook and the loops of your chain, allowing the loops to slip off the hook. Then tighten the newly formed stitch. Continue working one stitch in each chain until you have completed the full chain. This is called a slipstitch.

**Step K:** To end a chain or crocheted item, pull the wire through the last loop. Instead of creating an additional loop, enlarge the loop, then cut the wire, leaving an end. Pull tight.

When you work in wire, the wire is much stiffer than the yarn. It takes some practice to get consistency in your stitches. Begin with an inexpensive, flexible wire and gradually move up to precious metals.

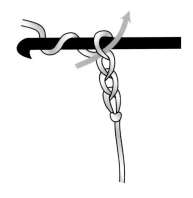

# CROCHETING WITH BEADS LARIAT

*With Jan Ketza Harris*

*Jan Ketza Harris: Crocheting with Beads Lariat. Courtesy of Galena Beads.*

This 6' 6" lariat necklace will be worn by folding it in half and pulling the tails through the loop. It can be worn either tight on the neck or loose upon the chest.

**Designer:** Jan Ketza Harris
**Finished Size:** 6' 6"
**Expense:** $50 to $100
**Expertise:** Intermediate
**Time to Complete:** A day

## Gathering Your Goods

20 lava 6mm rounds

21 raw amber 8mm to 12mm chunky cuts in irregular shapes

21 lipstick-red coral 10mm to 18mm chunky chips in irregular shapes

21 turquoise 10mm to 20mm chunky chips in irregular shapes

20 antique rose 6/0 seed beads

2 vintage 2" to 3" skeleton keys

Spool of 28-gauge natural copper color wire

**Where to Find:** Specialty bead stores; vintage shops; Knot Just Beads and Artistic Wire. (See Resource Guide, page 214.)

**Tools to Have on Hand**
Size G or H crochet hook
Wire cutter
Flat-nose pliers
Bead mat

*Buy strands of lava, red coral, raw amber and turquoise beads and select the most irregular shapes from the strands to create the most interesting lariat necklace.*

## TASK 1: STRINGING BEADS

To learn this technique you need to learn how to crochet the chain stitch. Practice with scrap yarn and a size G or H crochet hook. Once you get the basic stitch, do at least a 3' length for practice. It is easier to practice on yarn than the wire. See previous pages 154-155 for instructions.

*Using 28-gauge wire makes your wire crochet projects durable. It is strong enough to hold beads yet light enough for beautiful design. The Artistic Wire brand has nontarnish finishes. Sterling wire tarnishes and may be difficult to clean.*

**Step A:** Place your groups of beads in piles on your bead mat: Lava, turquoise, antique rose 6/0 seed beads, raw amber and red coral. This is the pattern you will use to string the beads onto the copper wire. All beads must be strung onto the wire before you start to crochet.

**Step B:** If you are right-handed, place the spool to the left side of your bead mat. You will be working the beads on the wire from the left to the right. You will need to have approximately 18" of wire released from the spool to start to crochet. Do not release more than this amount — you do not want to tangle unspooled wire.

**Step C:** Make a slip knot with the wire and place the crochet hook in the loop. Make three chains. Slide down the lava bead to the chains and hook the chain over the lava bead. Do two chains, slide down the turquoise bead and antique rose seed bead and chain over this group. Do two chains, slide down the raw amber and red coral beads and chain over. Do three chains, slide down the lava bead and chain over. Do two chains, slide down the turquoise bead and chain over. Do two chains, slide down the antique-rose seed bead and raw amber and chain over. Repeat this pattern 10 times. You will create a 6' length of wire crochet.

**Step D:** At the end of the last chain over, do three chains. Pull through the wire to secure the knot and cut off the wire, leaving a 4" length to create a tail for wrapping the keys off of the ends.

**TASK 2: ATTACHING THE KEYS**
**Step A:** To attach a key, take the tail of the end section, and put it through the key hole. Pull it through until a bead rests against the keyhole. Fold the chain section up and wire-wrap the tail around the next bead three times. With your wire cutter, trim extra wire.

**Step B:** Repeat with the other end of the tail and the other skeleton key. Wrap the wire three times and cut the extra wire.

# RETRO RAINBOW BAUBLES BELT

*With Wendy Mullane*

*Mackenzie Mullane: Retro Rainbow Baubles Belt. Courtesy of Vintaj Natural Brass Co.*

*This is such a fun way of designing. One of the best parts of this project is finding all of the vintage plastic beads and baubles at garage sales, thrift stores and flea markets! Ask your grandma if you can dig through her old bead and button jars.*

**Designer:** Mackenzie Mullane

**Finished Size:** 45"

**Expense:** Less than $25

**Expertise:** Beginner

**Time to Complete:** A day

## Tools to Have on Hand

J/10 6.0mm crochet hook

Round-nose pliers with side cutter

Chain-nose pliers (2 pair)

## Gathering Your Goods

20mm plastic bead

Natural brass 1½" headpin

35 assorted baubles and beads (found objects)

6 natural brass 1½" headpins

2 natural brass 6mm jump rings

12' of 1.5 hemp rope

**Where to Find:** Catalog suppliers; vintage shops; Vintaj Natural Brass Co. (See Resource Guide, page 214.)

## TASK 1: CREATING A COILED LOOP DROP

*Mackenzie Mullane: Retro Rainbow Baubles Belt. Courtesy of Vintaj Natural Brass Co.*

**Step A:** String the 20mm bead onto the 1½" headpin.

**Step B:** Holding the bead securely with your fingers, use the pliers to grip the straight end of the headpin. While still holding it securely, pull the headpin toward you. Bend it anywhere between a 45- and a 90-degree angle.

> *Coiling the end of the headpin is essential to ensuring that you'll have a secure dangle for attaching!*

**Step C:** Continue turning the headpin away from you (keeping the angle) until you've completed two full revolutions of a coiled loop, and achieved plenty of tension on the bead assemblage. Your bead should now be secure and your drop complete.

## TASK 2: PREPARING YOUR BEADS AND BAUBLES FOR STRINGING

**Step A:** Each bead or bauble needs a large-enough hole for the hemp to fit through. Try stringing each bead and removing it to see if the hole is large enough.

**Step B:** Separate the objects that fit on the hemp from the objects that don't. Set aside the objects that fit.

**Step C:** Sort the unfit objects into two piles. Pile No. 1 will have beads and objects with holes running through them, and Pile No. 2 will contain objects that have loops.

**Step D:** Create coiled loop drops for all of the beads or objects in Pile No. 1, using a 1½" headpin.

**Step E:** Attach a 6mm jump ring to all of the objects in Pile No. 2. Refer to the jump ring technique on page 137.

## TASK 3: STRINGING YOUR OBJECTS ONTO THE HEMP

**Step A:** Line up your beads and baubles in the order you'd like them to be on the belt.

**Step B:** String all 35 pieces onto the hemp.

## TASK 3: CROCHETING A BEADED BELT

**Step A:** Start about 6" from the end of the hemp. Make a slip knot — a loose single knot with a loop just large enough to slip the hook through — around the hook.

**Step B:** Wrap the hemp cord over the hook from back to front, between the hook end and the knot.

**Step C:** Draw the hemp cord through the loop. Repeat two stitches.

**Step D:** Crochet the next stitch around the first bead or bauble. Crochet four stitches. Crochet the fifth stitch around the next bead or bauble. Repeat 33 more times until all beads are crocheted into the belt. Stitches in between the beads can vary, depending upon the look you like.

**Step E:** Use your favorite knot technique to tie off both ends securely around the first and last bead on the belt. Your belt is now complete.

*Mackenzie Mullane: Retro Rainbow Baubles Belt. Courtesy of Vintaj Natural Brass Co.*

# MONK SPECIAL NECKLACE

*With Monique Roberson*

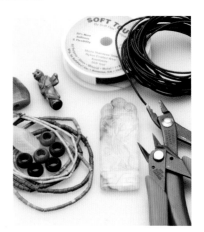

*Courtesy of Beadazzled. Photography by Cas Webber.*

You can create a wide variety of patterns using single knots.

**Designer:** Monique Roberson
**Finished Size:** 17"
**Expense:** $50 to $100
**Expertise:** Intermediate
**Time to Complete:** A day

### Tools to Have on Hand

Crimping pliers
Cutter

### Gathering Your Goods

Large serpentine pendant

Green 12mm serpentine leaf bead

Netsuke cat bead

Agate 12mm bead

115 brown 4mm tube block beads

100 coral 4mm tube block beads

50 turquoise 4mm block beads

10 crimps

Package of 1mm brown leather cord

Stringing material - (Medium Soft Flex Soft Touch was used in this project.)

**Where to Find:** Specialty bead stores

## TASK 1: CREATING A SQUARE KNOT

*Courtesy of Beadazzled.*
*Photography by Cas Webber.*

**Step A:** Place the outer right cord over the two middle cords and through the loop of the left outer cord. Then pull it tight.

**Step B:** Repeat Step A in reverse.

## TASK 2: CREATING AN OVERHAND KNOT

**Step A:** Create a loop using both cords in your hand.

**Step B:** Pull the top part of the cords through the loop and pull tight.

**Step C:** Repeat Step A and B again and again until you reach the desired lengths.

## TASK 3: MAKING YOUR NECKLACE

**Step A:** Cut three 8" pieces of stringing material.

*Courtesy of Beadazzled. Photography by Cas Webber.*

**Step B:** String 25 brown block beads on each strand. Then use nine coral block beads on either side on all three strands. Then add 10 turquoise block beads on either side on all three strands.

> A corkboard or foam core board serves as a nice place to work on your macramé knotting because you can pin it down as you go.

*Courtesy of Beadazzled. Photography by Cas Webber.*

**Step C:** Fold all three strands of stringing material in half, and feed them through the green leaf bead. This will create six ends that need to be individually crimped above the green bead.

*Courtesy of Beadazzled. Photography by Cas Webber.*

**Step D:** Use the inside indentation for the first crimp.

**Step E:** Use the outside indentation to round off the crimp.

*Courtesy of Beadazzled. Photography by Cas Webber.*

**Step F:** String one 24" leather cord through the loops of the six strands and add two wood beads. Create nine square knots and then finish with an overhand knot. Using the knotting techniques from pages 163 and 164. Do not cut the extra ends.

**Step G:** Cut two 8" pieces of stringing material.

**Step H:** String 18 brown block beads on each strand. Fold the strands in half and add one wood bead and one large agate bead. String eight coral block beads on all four strands and then add five turquoise beads on each of the four strands.

**Step I:** Add all of the strands through the Netsuke cat bead and crimp all four strands above the bead.

**Step J:** String one 24" piece of leather cord through the loops of the four strands and add two wood beads. Create nine square knots and an overhand knot at the end using the knotting techniques from pages 163 and 164. Do not cut off the extra ends.

## TASK 4: ADDING THE PENDANT AND FINISHING

*Courtesy of Beadazzled. Photography by Cas Webber.*

*Courtesy of Beadazzled. Photography by Cas Webber.*

**Step A:** Cut one 8" length of leather cord and string it through the hole of the pendant.

**Step B:** Create an overhand knot, and loop one tail in the left side of the necklace and one tail in the right side of the necklace.

**Step C:** Create an overhand knot above the first overhand knot. Cut the extra tails.

**Step D:** String the remaining extra leather pieces from both sides of the necklace through two wood beads, and tie overhand knots on each end.

*Courtesy of Beadazzled. Photography by Cas Webber.*

# TROPICAL GARDEN NECKLACE
*With Sandra Webster*

*Sandra Webster: Tropical Garden Necklace.*
*Courtesy of Sandra Webster Jewelry.*

**Designer:** Sandra Webster

**Other Contributor:** Barbara Svetlick of River of Glass Studio in Fort Lauderdale, Fla.

**Finished Size:** Adjustable 15" to 17", without clasp

**Expense:** More than $100

**Expertise:** Intermediate

**Time to Complete:** A day

## Gathering Your Goods

5mm freshwater pearls

Sterling silver double-bead tip findings

Red 1¾"-diameter lampwork flower

2 red 1"-diameter lampwork flowers

2 red ¾"-diameter lampwork flower buds

6 lime-green ½" lampwork leaves

4 textured earthtone 14 to 15mm lampwork focal beads

4 peridot-green 8mm faceted crystal beads

Strand of sage-green 6mm freshwater pearls

2 gold-filled double-cup bead tips

Handwrought gold-filled clasp made from 16-gauge gold-filled wire (or purchased clasp)

2" gold-filled extension chain

Gold-filled 2" headpin

Sage-green Griffin No. 6 silk beading cord

**Where to Find:** Catalog supplier; artisans

## Tools to Have on Hand

Flush cutter

Super Glue

Pliers

*You can use whatever beads you have on hand to learn the technique. Just be sure the beading cord fits through the holes in the beads.*

## TASK 1: MAKING HAND KNOTS

Hand knotting with silk will give you a quality-made, durable piece of jewelry that is supple and will drape beautifully around your neck.

*Hand knotting takes patience and practice. Work slowly. Your beads should end up evenly spaced and your knots should be as close as possible to the beads preceding them.*

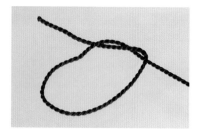

*Courtesy of Sandra Webster Jewelry.*

**Step A:** Tie an overhand knot at the end of the silk cord.

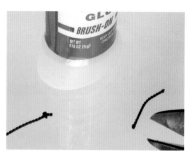

*Courtesy of Sandra Webster Jewelry.*

**Step B:** Cut close to the knot with a flush cutter, and dab the knot with glue.

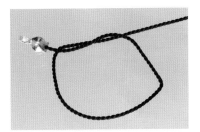

**Step C:** Add a double-bead tip and make another overhand loop. Using your thumb and forefinger, pinch the loop of the knot-to-be with your left hand. Work the loop of the beading thread down toward the bead tip until it is a couple of inches from it and about ½" in diameter. Then, using your right hand, work the loop next to the bead tip and tighten. The knot should be snug against the bead tip.

> Once you hand knot with silk cord, and you become familiar working with it, the knotting will become almost automatic.

## TASK 2: ADDING BEADS

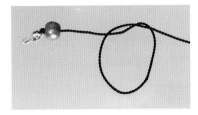

**Step A:** Slide a pearl onto the cord until it is snug against the bead tip. Tie another overhand knot and using your fingers, carefully slide the loop snugly against the pearl and tighten.

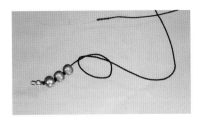

**Step B:** Repeat Step A until you have the desired length of hand knotting.

> It is easier to learn hand knotting if you start out working with waxed linen cord. It is heavier and stiffer than silk cord, so you may need to find beads with larger holes so that linen cord will fit through them.

## TASK 3: BEGINNING THE NECKLACE

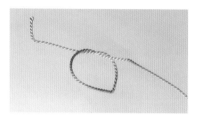

*Courtesy of Sandra Webster Jewelry.*

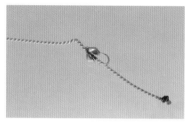

*Courtesy of Sandra Webster Jewelry.*

**Step A:** Tie an overhand knot at the end of the beading cord. Trim close to the knot with the cutter and dab the knot with glue.

**Step B:** Slide the needle end of the silk cord through the hole in the bead tip, entering the front side of the bead tip with the hook. Add one link of gold-filled chain, and close the tip of the bead tip. Add the clasp to the link of chain.

**Step C:** Tie another overhand knot, and slide it snugly against the bead tip. Use your fingers to guide the knots into place.

**Step D:** Add the first pearl, and tie another knot, sliding it snugly against the pearl. Continue until you have added your desired length of pearls. There is about 3" of hand knotted pearls on each side of this necklace.

## TASK 4: ADDING FLOWERS, LEAVES AND FOCAL LAMPWORK BEADS

*Courtesy of Sandra Webster Jewelry.*

*Courtesy of Sandra Webster Jewelry.*

**Step A:** String one lampwork leaf, 1" diameter lampwork flower, crystal bead, pearl, lampwork focal bead, pearl, lampwork leaf, two pearls and the large central lampwork flower.

**Step B:** Repeat Step A on the other side of the necklace, but add beads in reverse order.

**Step C:** Begin hand knotting pearls on the other side of the necklace until you have same length as the first side of the necklace.

**Step D:** After adding the last pearl, tie the final knot.

## TASK 5: FINISHING THE NECKLACE

*Courtesy of Sandra Webster Jewelry.*

*Courtesy of Sandra Webster Jewelry.*

**Step A:** Add a bead tip and tie another overhand knot, being careful to guide the knot into the bead-tip cup.

*NOTE:* I use my fingertips, but some people use an awl.

**Step B:** Dab the knot with glue, and trim close to the knot. Use pliers to close the cup over the knot.

*Courtesy of Sandra Webster Jewelry.*

*Courtesy of Sandra Webster Jewelry.*

**Step C:** Add the gold-filled extension chain, and close the tip.

**Step D:** Slide a couple of pearls onto the gold-filled headpin, and make a simple loop. Add it to the chain, and complete wrapping the loop. Add the clasp of your choice to the other side of the necklace.

# HAND-KNOTTED RIO NECKLACE

*With Sandra Webster*

*Sandra Webster: Rio Necklace Courtesy of Sandra Webster Jewelry.*

**Designer:** Sandra Webster

**Finished Size:** 20½" without clasp

**Expense:** More than $100

**Expertise:** Intermediate

**Time to Complete:** A day

## Gathering Your Goods

6 flat black 15mm wooden beads

5 lantern-shaped 12mm raffia beads

4 red-splatter 10mm x 15mm painted porcelain beads

7 assorted sterling silver beads in mixed sizes, shapes

5 turquoise 12mm round beads

2 turquoise 8mm round beads

Artisan focal 20mm lampwork bead

7 artisan assorted 6mm to 10mm lampwork beads

10 assorted small sterling beads

2 pewter or sterling rings (ring half of a toggle set) any size you like; shown approximately ½" in diameter

Sterling or pewter fishhook clasp of your choice

Waxed black linen 1mm cord

**Where to Find:** Suppliers; artisans

## Tools to Have on Hand

Cutter

Permanent Glue

## TASK 1: ATTACH ONE END RING

**Step A:** Cut two lengths of linen cord, each 12' long. Fold each in half. You will be working with a doubled strand of cord for each strand of this necklace.

*Courtesy of Sandra Webster Jewelry.*

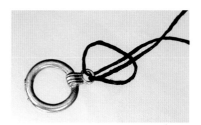

*Courtesy of Sandra Webster Jewelry.*

**Step B:** Take the end of the doubled cord that has a "loop" in it, and string it through the hole of the ring that will be the end of the necklace. Loop the other ends of the cord through the loop, and pull tight. You are now ready to start hand knotting beads onto the cords.

**Step C:** Following the instructions for the Hand-Knotting Technique on page 170, make your first knot with the doubled cord. Add a bead and make another knot. Leave a ½" space, and make another knot. Add the next bead, and continue the process. Place the beads in an order that will be pleasing to the eye.

*Courtesy of Sandra Webster Jewelry.*

**Step D:** If you have a bead that will not allow both cords to pass through, just pass one cord through the bead. Lay the other cord around the bead, and tie a knot, making a "cradle" for the bead. Leave a little room for the beads to move about a bit, or place the knots tight against the beads, if you prefer.

## TASK 2: ATTACHING THE RING TO THE OTHER END OF THE NECKLACE

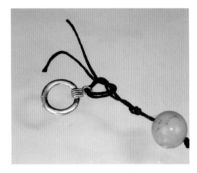

*Courtesy of Sandra Webster Jewelry.*

**Step A:** When the longest strand of the necklace is the length you want, you are ready to add the other ring to the end of the necklace. Pass both cords through the small "connector" ring on the toggle clasp and tie a square knot by creating a simple overhand knot. The first strand of this necklace is 23" long.

**Step B:** Trim close to the knot and dab the cut edge with glue.

## TASK 3: MAKING THE SHORTER STRAND OF THE NECKLACE

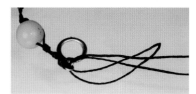

*Courtesy of Sandra Webster Jewelry.*

**Step A:** Using the other piece of linen cord, fold it in half as you did the first one. Attach it to one of the rings on the ends of the necklace using the technique from Task 2, page 178.

*Courtesy of Sandra Webster Jewelry.*

**Step B:** Tie a knot, and begin adding beads. Keep the spacing the same as on the first strand. Also, note the colors and sizes of beads on the first strand.

**Step C:** Continue adding beads and knotting them in place until the second strand is 19" long, excluding rings.

*Courtesy of Sandra Webster Jewelry.*

**Step D:** Attach the cord to the ring using another square knot. Trim the knot, and dab with glue. Attach the clasp of your choice to one of the rings.

# EARTH, SUN AND SKY NECKLACE

*With Deborah McClintock*

*Deborah McClintock: Earth, Sun & Sky Necklace. Courtesy of Beadazzled. Photography by Cas Webber.*

**Designer:** Deborah McClintock
**Expense:** $50-$75
**Expertise:** Beginner-Intermediate

## Gathering Your Goods

Strand of turquoise chips
Strand of coral chips
Brown No. 6 silk cord
Coffee mug
2 Southwest-style sterling silver cones

## Gathering Your Goods (continued)

Sterling silver hook-and-eye clasp
2 pieces 20-gauge sterling silver wire, 3" long

## Tools to Have on Hand

Knotting tweezers
Bead stoppers (substitute a hemostat if desired)
Ruler
Round-nose pliers
Chain-nose pliers
Wire cutter
Bead cement

## TASK 1: PRE-STRETCHING THE SILK CORD

**Step A:** Take the cord completely off of the card. Do not remove the wire attached to one end, this will act as a needle.

**Step B:** Tie both ends of the silk cord to a coffee mug.

**Step C:** Hang the cord over a door for 24 hours. This prevents the silk from stretching later as you wear it, which will cause the beads to become loose.

## TASK 2: KNOTTING BEADS ON CORD

This technique will teach you how to create a "floating" bead necklace.

*Courtesy of Beadazzled.*
*Photography by Cas Webber.*

**Step B:** Slide on the first bead, then make another overhand knot, keeping the loop loose.

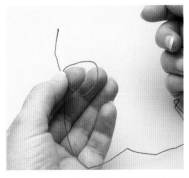

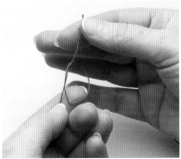

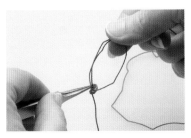

*Courtesy of Beadazzled.*
*Photography by Cas Webber.*

**Step A:** Tie an overhand knot about 4" from the end of the cord by making a loop and pulling the end of the silk through the loop. Pull to tighten.

*Courtesy of Beadazzled.*
*Photography by Cas Webber.*

**Step C:** Insert the tweezers inside the loop (think of diving into a pool) and grasp the cord at the top of the bead.

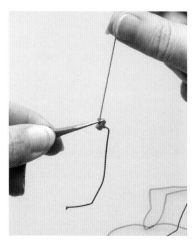

*Courtesy of Beadazzled.*
*Photography by Cas Webber.*

*Courtesy of Beadazzled.*
*Photography by Cas Webber.*

**Step D:** Pull the cord tight. The knot will form around the tweezers. Gently remove the tweezers without opening them.

**Step E:** Starting about ½" from the knot, place the tweezers on the cord. Gently move them down the cord toward the knot while pulling up on the cord with your other hand. This tightens the knot against the bead.

## TASK 3: ADDING BEADS

**NOTE:** When you need to leave a space between the beads, you will need a bead stopper, or hemostat to knot against.

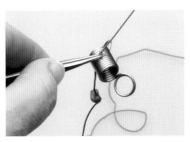

*Courtesy of Beadazzled.*
*Photography by Cas Webber.*

**Step A:** Using a ruler, measure the distance you want to leave between the last bead and the next bead.

**Step B:** Place the bead stopper, or hemostat in the desired location, and knot as if you were knotting against a bead. Add a bead and continue.

**Step C:** Continue adding beads and knotting between them as shown in the photo, or as desired.

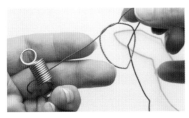

*Courtesy of Beadazzled.*
*Photography by Cas Webber.*

*It is important to place the tweezers inside the loop you make, on top of your bead, and pull the silk tight. If you place the tweezers under the loop, the knot won't form where you want it.*

## TASK 4: MAKING A WRAPPED EYE LOOP

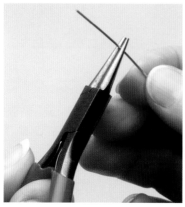

*Courtesy of Beadazzled.*
*Photography by Cas Webber.*

**Step B:** Place the round-nose pliers ¼" from the bend.

*Courtesy of Beadazzled.*
*Photography by Cas Webber.*

**Step A:** Starting about ¾" from one end of the wire, bend it to a 90-degree angle with the round-nose pliers.

*Courtesy of Beadazzled.*
*Photography by Cas Webber.*

**Step C:** Place the hand holding the pliers palm up, and bend the wire around to form a circle, keeping the pliers inside the loop.

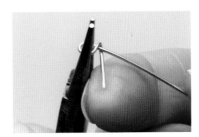

*Courtesy of Beadazzled.*
*Photography by Cas Webber.*

**Step D:** With the other hand, grasp the end of the wire and, wrap it around the base of the loop two or three times.

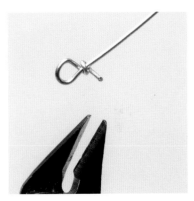

*Courtesy of Beadazzled.*
*Photography by Cas Webber.*

**Step E:** Using the wire cutter, trim the excess wire.

## TASK 5: TYING THE SILK CORDS ONTO THE WRAPPED EYE LOOP

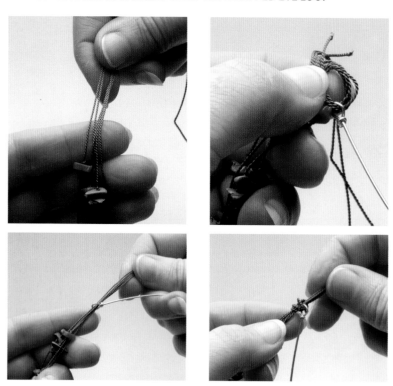

*Courtesy of Beadazzled. Photography by Cas Webber.*

**Step A:** Gather together the ends of the silk cords and tie them onto the wrapped eye loop using a square knot. See page 163 for directions on making a square knot.

## TASK 6: ADDING A CONE AND CLASP

*Courtesy of Beadazzled.*
*Photography by Cas Webber.*

**Step A:** Slide the cone over the wire; pull the wire into the cone as far as it will go.

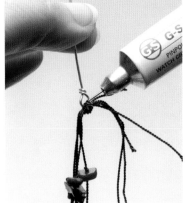

*Courtesy of Beadazzled.*
*Photography by Cas Webber.*

**Step B:** Apply bead cement to the knot.

**Step C:** When the glue is dry, trim the end of the silk. It doesn't need to look pretty. This will be inside the cone.

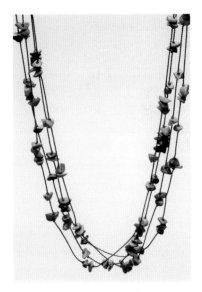

*Courtesy of Beadazzled.*
*Photography by Cas Webber.*

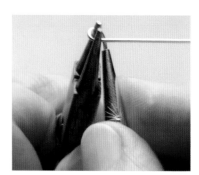

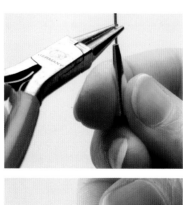

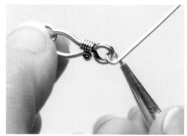

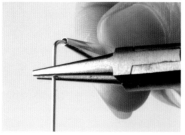

*Courtesy of Beadazzled. Photography by Cas Webber.*

**Step B:** With the wire extending from the top of the cone, make another wrapped eye loop. Before you wrap the wire, open the loop slightly using the chain-nose pliers, and slip the loop end of the hook clasp inside the loop.

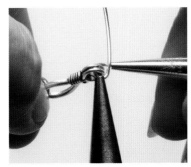

*Courtesy of Beadazzled.*
*Photography by Cas Webber.*

**Step C:** Finish wrapping the wire two or three times until it is tight against the cone.

*Courtesy of Beadazzled.*
*Photography by Cas Webber.*

**Step D:** Using the wire cutter, trim the excess wire. Using the chain-nose pliers, press the end down so it doesn't create a sharp point.

**Step E:** Repeat with the other half of the clasp.

When tying the silk onto the wrapped eye loop, make sure there is a cluster of beads very near the knot. This will look better when you pull the cord into the cone.

When making the wrapped eye loop at the top of the cone, leave about ⅛" between the top of the cone and the bend in the wire to accommodate the wrapped wire.

# CRYSTAL ELEGANCE NECKLACE

*With Christy Nicholas*

*Christy Nicholas: Crystal Elegance.*

**Designer:** Christy Nicholas/ Green Dragon

**Finished Size:** 18" long

**Expense:** $25 to $50

**Expertise:** Beginner

**Time to Complete:** An evening

## Gathering Your Goods

Several 6mm bicone crystals

Several 11/0 seed beads or Delica beads

Commercial magnetic clasp

224 bicone 6mm beads

10 grams 11/0 Delica or seed beads

One commercial clasp finding

Nymo thread (or any similar thread)

**Where to Find:** Mass merchants; specialty bead stores; catalog suppliers

## Tools to Have on Hand

Beading needle

Scissors

Bead tray or bead board

## TASK 1: TUBULAR PEYOTE STITCH, STRINGING TO FORM A RING

**Step A:** Cut about 3' of beading thread (for making several rings), and thread the needle.

**Step B:** You will use an even number (four to eight) of both the bicones and the seed beads. String the beads in this order: bicone, seed, bicone, seed, bicone, seed, bicone, seed, until all are strung.

*Courtesy of Christy Nicholas.*

**Step C:** Pass the needle through the first bicone strung, going the same direction you initially passed the needle through to form a ring.

## TASK 2: FORMING THE SECOND CRYSTAL RING

**Step A:** For this step you, will use an odd number (three to seven of each) of bicones and seed beads.

**Step B:** With the thread coming out of one of the seed beads from the first crystal ring, string the beads in the following order: bicone, seed, bicone, seed, bicone, seed, until you have strung all the beads. The last bead on the thread should be a bicone.

**Step C:** Thread the needle through the seed bead prior to the one you came out of in the first crystal ring. This forms the second ring.

**Step D:** Continue passing the thread through the next bicone (on the first ring) and the original seed bead you came out of.

*Courtesy of Christy Nicholas.*

## TASK 3: ATTACHING A CLASP

**Step A:** Cut about 2' of beading thread, and thread the needle.

**Step B:** Secure your thread within your project, near the end where you want the clasp attached. Weave the thread in and out of the beads several times so it is secure.

**Step C:** String five seed beads onto your thread, one side of the magnetic clasp, and then string five more seed beads to your needle.

**Step D:** With the threaded needle, go back into the end of your project, weaving the thread in and out of the project several times to make sure it is secure. Repeat the steps on the other end of the project.

*Christy Nicholas: Crystal Elegance.*

## TASK 4: MAKING A CRYSTAL RING CHAIN

**Step A:** Form a four-bicone crystal ring. This will be one end of the necklace and will be attached to the clasp.

**Step B:** Attach six more four-bicone crystal rings to the first, one after another, forming a chain.

**Step C:** Attach a six-bicone crystal ring to the last ring created in Step B.

**Step D:** Attach eight more six-bicone crystal rings to Step Cs crystal ring.

**Step E:** Attach an eight-bicone crystal ring to the last ring created in Step D.

*Courtesy of Christy Nicholas.*

**Step F:** Attach five more eight-bicone crystal rings to the ring created in Step E.

## TASK 5: CREATING THE SECOND SIDE OF THE NECKLACE

**Step A:** Repeat Task 4, Step A through Step E, to form the second side of the necklace.

**Step B:** Attach two more eight-bicone crystal rings to the ring created in Step E from Task 4.

> *Throughout your design, you may want to occasionally tie a small knot in the thread between beads to secure the design. The more often you do this, the more stable and secure the design will be.*

**Step C:** When forming the next bicone crystal ring, use the fourth eight-bicone crystal ring from Task 4 as one of the crystals.

**Step D:** With your thread coming out of one seed bead, string bicone, seed, bicone, seed, bicone, seed, bicone, seed, bicone onto the thread.

**Step E:** Thread the needle through the seed, bicone, seed from the other crystal ring (the fourth eight-bicone ring in Task 5) that is on the "side" of the ring when held up vertically.

**Step F:** Add another bicone, and then finish up the crystal ring by threading through the previous ring's seed, bicone, seed.

### TASK 6: FORMING THE "V"

**Step A:** Complete two more eight-bicone crystal rings as in Step C from Task 5, attaching them to the previous side's eight-bicone crystal rings. This should form a V in the necklace.

*Courtesy of Christy Nicholas.*

**Step B:** At the bottom of the V, add a four-bicone ring using the two center bottom crystals.

*Photo courtesy of Christy Nicholas.*

**Step C:** Form two more four-bicone rings, each using a crystal from the four-bicone ring in Step B above..

# STARRY NIGHT CHOKER

*With Cristy Nicholas*

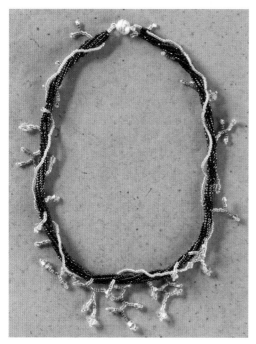

*Christy Nicholas: Starry Night Choker.*
*Photo courtesy of Christy Nicholas.*

**Designer:** Christy Nicholas
**Finished Size:** 16" long
**Expense:** Less than $25
**Expertise:** Intermediate
**Time to Complete:** A day

*Delicas work better than seed beads in this project, as they show off the distinctive her-ringbone pattern of the tube more. Seed beads can be used, however, if desired.*

## Gathering Your Goods

25 g 11/0 Delica beads

Swarovski 6mm crystal beads (as desired)

1 g 11/0 seed beads (as desired)

Square beads (as desired)

Bicone crystals or others (as desired)

5 g seed beads

Commercial clasp finding

Nymo thread, size D (or any similar thread)

**Where to Find:** Mass merchants; Specialty bead stores

## Tools to Have on Hand

Beading needle

Bead tray or bead board

Scissors

## TASK 1: CREATING A TUBE FOR A CHOKER

**Step A:** Cut a piece of beading thread about 4' long in the color you want to make the tube, and thread the needle.

**Step B:** String four Delica beads onto the thread.

**Step D:** Continue going around through the second two beads, so you have almost made a complete double circle through the four beads.

**Step E:** Add two more Delica beads to the thread.

*Photo courtesy of Christy Nicholas.*

**Step F:** Go through the second two beads in the same direction you did the first time. Your beads should now form three sets of two beads in a row.

**Step G:** Repeat method until you have six sets of two beads.

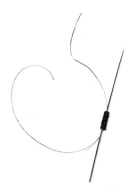

*Photo courtesy of Christy Nicholas.*

**Step C:** Go back through the first two beads in the same direction you initially went through and form a loop.

## TASK 2: BUILDING A TUBE

*Photo courtesy of Christy Nicholas.*

**Step A:** Once you have six sets of two beads, you need to connect them into a circle. Instead of adding two more beads, pass the needle through the first two beads you added, and come back through the last two you added. You should now have a circle of beads, two deep, six around. This is your "base" for the tube.

**Step B:** Add two beads to your thread.

**Step C:** Pass your needle down through the next "base" bead from the one your thread is emerging from, to form a miniature loop.

**Step D:** Pass your needle up through the next base bead from the one your thread is emerging from so your thread comes up from the base, to the left of your loop.

**Step E:** Repeat Steps B through D two more times. You should now have a new row of six beads on top of your original two base rows of six beads.

**Step F:** Bring your needle up through the right bead of one of the three loops, and repeat Task 1, Steps A through C three more times.

**Step G:** Repeat Steps B through F enough times to create a tube the length as desired.

To attach a clasp, see page 191 for more information. For chokers, magnetic clasps work well as they require little dexterity for attaching and detaching.

**NOTE:** When creating the tube, you will notice that it is squishy — that is part of the nature of this design. However, to reduce the looseness, be sure to keep the stitches tight as you work through this project.

> *Throughout your design, you may want to occasionally tie a small knot in the thread between beads to secure the design. The more you do this, the more stable the design will be.*

## TASK 3: ADDING A SWIRLING LINE TO A TUBE

*You can use this on any tube of beads created, be it peyote, square stitch or others. If you use it with a tube that naturally swirls in one direction, it has a dramatic effect if the swirling line goes in the opposite direction of the tube.*

**Step A:** Cut a piece of thread about 4' long in the color you want to make the line, and thread the needle.

**Step B:** Secure the thread on one end of the tube.

**Step C:** String seven seed beads onto the thread.

**Step D:** From where your thread emerges, count six beads up and two beads over on the tube. This is your first anchor bead.

**Step E:** Pass the needle through the anchor bead, then back toward the end you started from.

**Step F:** Pass the needle through the last seed bead strung, going in the same direction you did the first time. This secures the first section of your line.

**Step G:** Repeat Steps D through G until you come to the other end of the tube.

## TASK 4: ADDING BRANCHES TO A TUBE

*You can use this on any tube of beads created. The branches can be short, long, many or few, depending on your desired result and look. Each branch can have crystals, square beads, triangle beads or just seed beads. You can have a regular feel or a wild one. For a wilder look, space your branches randomly around the tube.*

*Photo courtesy of Christy Nicholas.*

**Step A:** Cut a piece of thread about 4' long in the color you want to make the branch, and thread the needle.

**Step B:** Secure the thread on one end of the tube.

**Step C:** Come down through the beads in the tube until you are at a spot to secure your first branch. You can have as many branches as you like.

**Step D:** Add seven beads to the thread.

**Step E:** Skipping the seventh bead, go back through the last three beads, so you have a branch sticking out.

**Step F:** Add seven more beads to the thread.

**Step G:** Repeat Step E.

**Step H:** Thread the needle back down to the base bead, and into the beads of the tube itself.

**Step I:** Emerge at the next spot you wish to attach a branch.

**Step J:** Repeat Steps C through I until you come to the other end of the tube.

**Step K:** See the instructions on page 192 for more information on attaching clasps.

# CHAPTER NINE

## COMMUNITY

# BECOMING PART OF THE COMMUNITY

Beading can be life-changing.

Become part of your local beading community and share your talents with family, friends and even new acquaintances:

- Make gifts for friends.

- Teach beading to a young lady and watch her confidence grow.

- See a young mother on a tight budget, with as little as $10, make a beautiful bracelet she will treasure always (a little deserved bling!).

- Laugh and share good times with young and old friends and family while beading together.

- Help a new father make a special gift for a surprised and happy wife.

- Give your team spirit a boost with bracelets made of team colors.

- Teach residents at the local women's shelter to find happiness and hope in a new skill.

- Make "get well" prayer bracelets for an ill friend.

- Create a jewelry ensemble for a new bride and her bridesmaids.

- Help your youth council or your religious group start a fundraiser selling fabulous earrings or jewelry.

- Give a middle-aged woman her first adventure into her own creativity as she finds her own voice for the first time.

- Make friends with designers around the world while sharing tips and techniques.

Once you've gained a passion for creating jewelry, your friends and acquaintances will likely begin to ask you if they can buy it from you! Before you know it, you will be forming your own "community" of jewelry enthusiasts. From the clerk at the specialty bead store where you purchase your beads to the teller at your local bank who can't wait to purchase your latest creation, your beading community will grow and grow.

If you are intent on expanding your bead collection and selling your work, there are a few things you should consider.

*Ilene Baranowitz: Crystal Gilded Evening Bag with Beaded Tassel.*

## TIPS FOR DESIGNING YOUR OWN JEWELRY AND SELLING YOUR WORK WITH ILENE BARANOWITZ

**Start by believing in yourself:**

- *Be confident.*
- *Find your inner voice.*
- *Be courageous. If not now, when?*

### How do you come up with the best designs?

- *Look around you — what would you really like to have yourself?*
- *What do you need that you can't find?*
- *Does it exist already? If so, can you think of a way it could be better?*
- *Is it something you absolutely can't live without, now that you have identified it?*
- *Check the Web.*
- *Browse the aisles of the major craft retailers.*
- *Visit your local bead stores often.*
- *Keep a journal of your discoveries and ideas.*

### Research, research, research!

- *Visit the library.*
- *"Google it" on the Web.*
- *Shop 'til you drop.*
- *Be a sponge and absorb everything you possibly can.*
- *Keep your mind open and the ideas will start to come to you.*

**Plan Your Presentation:**

- Draw out your ideas.
- Create a digital presentation.
- Make prototypes.
- Make a list of the pros and cons, and then check it twice. Eliminate materials and associated ideas that won't work well. Key in on those that have potential.
- Consider ways to save costs and add value for the consumer.
- Consider what markup will work best for you and your store owner. Be realistic. You want your jewelry to sell well.
- Evaluate ways you can help to market your designs. Be on-hand for major store events, offer a trunk show to preview new jewelry, and meet the customers. You will learn more about what consumers like and dislike about your designs during these one-on-one opportunities.
- Make friends and enjoy your journey.

**When approaching a potential buyer:**

- Take a deep breath.
- Close your eyes and imagine your success.
- Remember the four Cs: Cool, Clear, Collected and Confident.
- While keeping your feet on the ground, there is a fine balance, which you will learn over time. Speak slowly, confidently and clearly when conveying your thoughts.

**Once you have found a good match:**

- Keep names, addresses and phone numbers on index cards for easy access.
- Does the buyer have a Web site? Visit it.
- Write down a summary of your discussion: terms to consider, store policies, etc.
- Follow up on sales and replenishment.

# FINANCIAL CONSIDERATIONS:

Inquire at your state and city offices about a resale license for beads and supplies. Local bead stores (and some national chains) offer discounts to resellers. Once you have your resale tax number (it is as easy as filling out a retailer's tax form) you will get the discounts in many instances. Requirements vary from store to store, city to city and state to state, so be sure to check locally. Also inquire about collecting and remitting sales taxes on your sales. Get advice from your accountant and attorney.

If your quantities are large enough, you can inquire directly to the vendor or importer about setting up a wholesale account to buy your beads. It is important to keep track of your costs, so that you will know how to price your jewelry pieces to make the most profit.

### CREATE YOUR OWN BLING
By Ilene Baranowitz

*Crystal-embellished items are hotter than ever, but those elegant evening clutches can put a serious strain on your bank account. Now you can personalize your accessories with style — and look like a million dollars.* **Create Your Own Bling** *shows you how to turn purses and accessories into dazzling fashion statements.*

# SEIZING THE OPPORTUNITIES

*Barbara Carleton: Sunstone Cascade Necklace.*

Some local shop owners might allow you to consign jewelry in their shops or may buy pieces of jewelry from you outright. Just remember, they must make money, too, and they will also mark up the price of your work. Traditionally, consignments range from 20 percent to 40 percent of the retail price. Retailers usually make 45 to 65 percent of the retail price when they buy goods to sell outright. Each time the jewelry is marked up, it puts a burden on the consumer, so be certain you don't price yourself out of the market. Look for good values when buying supplies.

There are many opportunities to sell your work. Local craft fairs will help acquaint you with your marketplace. You can experiment with styles to see what sells and how to best display your work and you can spend some time with customers to find out more about what appeals to them.

At local craft shows, you have an opportunity to offer the consumer the best value by selling your work yourself. Your customers get to meet you, the designer, which is always a plus. Save a list of your best customers so you can let them know when you have a new collection previewing. Postcard mailings or e-mails are good marketing tools. Art guilds sometimes have galleries (some take as little as 20 percent of the retail price for commission). Ask other jewelry designers about their experiences. Many are willing to share, and you can learn a great deal from their successes.

Find a mentor. Someone who has had success in the marketplace and is willing to guide you is a tremendous asset.

Many designers have turned to the Internet to reach a broader market and retain the "direct sales" route. Whether you choose a general merchant or auction like eBay.com or amazon. com, or a specialty site that caters to a specific market, you must be willing to put time and energy into your Web experience. You can also create your own Web site. Take into consideration the time and money to build, maintain and market your site. Pass out business cards or brochures with your Web address on them to help those interested in your work. It is important to make every effort to let people know where to find you on the Web.

Some designers teach jewelry making and sell their work to their students, friends and families. Libraries and banks sometimes will allow you to exhibit your work, but they won't sell it for you. This is another instance when a business card or brochure will help you get the sale. You can host a home party to help get you started or have "previews" of new work in your home by invitation only.

This is a journey of community. It is a journey you can make even from a comfy chair in your living room. The choice is yours, the experiences full and the memories many. Share your enthusiasm, and it will change your life. Whatever road you travel, you will find rewarding friendships along the way.

Happy travels and best wishes on your journey.

— Susan Ray

# THE RICHNESS OF COMMUNITY

*With Penelope Diamanti*

Pioneer bead researcher Pete Francis reminded his students: "It's about the people." Pete knew all of the technical details of making beads, analyses of materials and excavating practices, but he found that to fully understand beads we need to understand the cultures involved. Their histories, economies, spiritual traditions and even politics have influenced the making, trading and wearing of beads through the ages.

Beads connect people across time, space, language, race, religion and just about anything that might divide us. Some appreciate their subtle colors and patinas; some respect their age and rarity; others gravitate toward their symbolism; and a few examine them for clues to their construction. Whatever pulls us in, once we've been caught in the orbit of beads, it's almost impossible to escape.

Our community consists of several interrelated groups: beadmakers, bead traders, designers using beads and bead researchers. It starts with a diverse group of beadmakers: lost-wax brass casters of the Ivory Coast; powder-glass beadmakers of Ghana in West Africa; clay beadmakers in Peru; silver beadmakers in India, Indonesia and Thailand; and American and Japanese contemporary glass beadmakers, among others.

# Adventures of a Lifetime
## ABOUT PENELOPE DIAMANTI, OWNER OF BEADAZZLED, INC. IN VIRGINIA, MARYLAND AND WASHINGTON, D.C.

The first traders Penelope met were Hausa vendors from Nigeria who presided over stalls in the Treichville Market in Abidjan, Ivory Coast, where she got hooked on beads. She visited the market almost daily, learning about bargaining — and about loyalties and economics. As tourists found their way into the market, Penelope saw them sometimes being charged high prices. She learned the traders felt the tourists had not earned the lower prices they offered to her, a "local" who bought from them every week in increasing quantities. By charging tourists more, it enabled the traders to charge regulars like her less. This was her first lesson on wholesale vs. retail.

It wasn't long before Penelope applied the lesson, when she became a bead trader herself. She returned to the United States with a tin safari trunk full of beads and began peddling them to fellow students, making and selling jewelry to friends, consigning to small boutiques, and vending at craft fairs and shows around the West.

As a passionate collector and designer, Penelope states that she couldn't have a better job than buying and selling beads. The opportunity to meet makers and users of beads in a variety of cultures on four continents has greatly increased her understanding of their production, history and meaning.

*Courtesy of Beadazzled. Photography by William L. Allen.*

Penelope is committed to sharing what she has learned through the educational programs of her stores, her Web site (www.Beadazzled.net), her publications, including *Beadazzled: Where Beads & Inspiration Meet*, and through her work with the Bead Society of Greater Washington and the Bead Museum. Her hope is to be able to continue to support and inspire designers, collectors, students of bead history and entrepreneurs worldwide.

*Many of the designs in this book were prepared and photographed through the grace and generosity of Penelope Diamanti.*

## About the Photographer: William L. Allen

Photographer William L. (Bill) Allen served as the editor-in-chief of *National Geographic* for 10 years. During his 35-year career, he covered the world, producing hundreds of magazine articles and books as a photographer, writer or editor on topics ranging from the discovery of the Titanic to 21st-century slavery. Under his leadership, *National Geographic* earned numerous top magazine awards and dealt with important topics such as weapons of mass destruction, global warming and controversy over evolution.

He continues his interest in world cultures — and photography — through photographing beads and artwork as well as teaching digital photography and creativity at photography workshops. He serves on several boards of directors and resides in Alexandria, Va., when he can't find an excuse to be visiting Hawaii or fly-fishing.

More information is available at his Web site, www.billallenphotography.com.

*Courtesy of Beadazzled. Photography by William L. Allen.*

## About the Photographer: Cas Webber

Over the last 20 years, Cas Webber has lived and worked in Baltimore City and earned a Bachelors of Fine Arts degree in photography and performing arts in 1992. Cas has found that creative diversity and freedom have been her life's passions. Whether she is building for a props and sets company, custom painting, rehabbing her house, teaching jewelry classes, designing jewelry, shooting commercially, managing Baltimore's Beadazzled store or traveling for beads, she is always involved in a creative endeavor.

Her current assignments have focused on expanding her photography career while collaborating with businesses and craftspeople to visually introduce their products and brand their styles in the marketplace.

# About the Author: Susan Ray

Susan Ray has more than 30 years of experience in the fashion and craft industry as author, buyer and merchandise manager, and vice president of product and Web site development for companies including Peck & Peck, Frederick Atkins of New York, Ben Franklin retail stores, Jo-Ann Fabrics and IdeaForest.

She has spent years traveling to the Far East to develop proprietary products for retailers throughout the country. The strength of Susan's entrepreneurial spirit has attracted many companies to use her expertise in formulating new store concepts.

She was co-founder of a group of award-winning children's computer exploration facilities that received a ComputerWorld Smithsonian Award for innovation of technology.

Susan lives with her husband, Kevin Duhme, on their dairy farm in Maquoketa, Iowa. She is co-author of The *Art & Soul of Glass Beads*, 2003, *Easy Beaded Jewelry*, 2004, and most recently, she wrote *Organic Beaded Jewelry*, 2005.

In recent years she has celebrated the marriage of her son, Eric, to his wife, Velvette, who now shares Susan's passion for beading. Susan's jewelry, craft and interior designs have been featured in numerous national publications including *Better Homes and Gardens* and *Woman's Day* magazines.

*Visit Susan at her Web site:*
*www.beadasimplelife.com*

*Susan Ray: Magic Necklace.*

# RESOURCE GUIDE

Recommended Suppliers:

### Arrow Springs
www.ArrowSprings.com
4301 A Product Drive
Shingle Springs, CA 95682
800-899-0689

### Artistic Wire Ltd.
www.artisticwire.com
752 N. Larch Ave.
Elmhurst, IL 60126
630-530-7567
sales@artisticwire.com

### Ashes to Beauty Adornments
115 Camino de las Huertas
Placitas, NM 87043
505-867-4244

### Beadazzled
www.beadazzled.net
1507 Connecticut Ave. N.W.
Washington, D.C. 20036
202-265-2323

### Bejeweled Software Co.
www.jewelrydesignermanager.com
P.O. Box 430
Poway, CA 92074
858-679-3240
info@jewelrydesignermanager.com

### Cas Webber Photography
www.caswebber.com
CasWebber@mac.com

### The Clay Store
www.theclaystore.com
1255 Belle Ave., Suite 122
Winter Springs, FL 32708
877-602-0700
407-695-0429
info@theclaystore.com

### The Coiling Gizmo/The Refiner's Fire
www.coilinggizmo.com
P.O. Box 66612
Portland, OR 97290
503-775-5242
sales@coilinggizmo.com

### Fire Mountain Gems
www.firemountaingems.com
One Fire Mountain Way
Grants Pass, OR 97526
800-423-2319
questions@firemtn.com

### Frantz Art Glass & Supply
www.frantzartglass.com
130 W. Corporate Road
Shelton, WA 98584
800-839-6712

### Galena Beads
www.galenabeads.com
109 N. Main St.
Galena, IL 61036
815-777-4080

### JudiKins Inc.
www.judikins.com
17803 S. Harvard Blvd.
Gardena, CA 90248
310-515-1115
customerservice@judikins.com

**Just Leonardo**
www.leonardolampwork.com
362 Hood School Road
Indiana, PA 15701
724-357-8709
eBay ID: justleonardo

**Knot Just Beads**
www.knotjustbeads.com

**McKenzie Glassworks**
20818 Tiger Tail Road
Grass Valley, CA 95949
530-346-2068
www.mckenzieglassworks.com

**Christy Nicholas, (*Green Dragon*)**
www.GreenDragonArtist.com
6434 N.W. 32 St.
Gainesville, FL 32653
352-271-8477
GreenDragon@bellsouth.net
eBay ID: GrenDragn

**Northstar Glassworks**
www.northstarglass.com
9386 S.W. Tigard St.
Tigard, OR 97223
866-684-6986

**Polyform Products Co.**
www.polyformproducts.com
1901 Estes Ave.
Elk Grove Village, IL 60007
info@polyformproducts.com

**Rio Grande**
www.riogrande.com
7500 Bluewater Road N.W.
Albuquerque, NM 87121
800-545-6566

**Sandra Webster Jewelry**
www.sandrawebsterjewelry.com
5217 Old Spicewood Spg. Rd. No. 2003
Austin, TX 78731
800-934-9335
rwebster1@austin.rr.com

**School of Beadwork**
www.schoolofbeadwork.com
P.O. Box 4625
San Luis Obispo, CA 93403
805-440-613
sales@schoolofbeadwork.com

**Shutterfly**
www.shutterfly.com
3180 Corporate Place
Hayward, CA 94545

**Vintaj Natural Brass Co.**
*NOTE:* The company's Web site sells to whole-
salers and has a locator for retail outlets.
www.vintaj.com
P.O. Box 246
Galena, IL 61036
info@vintaj.com

**WigJig**
www.wigjig.com
P.O. Box 5124
Gaithersburg, MD 20882
800-579-WIRE
custsrv@wigiig.com

# CONTRIBUTORS

**William L. Allen**
P.O. Box 7410
Alexandria, VA 22307
202-374-3939
allenngs@earthlink.net

**Ilene Baranowitz**
1953 Lake Brook Circle
Dandridge, TN 37725
865-397-3880
ibaran@comcast.net

**Tracy Callahan**
311 Cedarwood Court
Russellville, AR 72801
479-858-2113
tracyc@cox-internet.com
eBay ID: TracyC1959

**Sherrie Chapin**
**Blue Moon Jewelry**
www.bluemoonjewelry.com
White Bear Lake, MN
651-503-5820
mail@bluemoonjewelry.com

**Rene M. Chock**
**Ashes to Beauty Adornments**
115 Camino de las Huertas
Placitas, NM 87043
505-867-4244

**Joyce S. Diamanti**
**Penelope Diamanti**
**Beadazzled, Inc.**
www.beadazzled.net
1507 Connecticut Ave. N.W.
Washington, D.C.
202-265-2323

*Jeanne Holland: Springs and Things*
*Industrial Elegance.*

**Eileen Feldman**
**Beautiful Inspirations**
**By EF Designs**
3604 Berdan Ave.
Fairlawn, NJ 07410
201-321-6583
eileensf@optonline.net

**LeRoy Goertz**
**The Refiner's Fire**
www.leroygoertz.com
P.O. Box 66612
Portland, OR 97290
503-775-5242
info@coilinggizmo.com

**Gary L. Helwig**
**WigJig**
www.wigjig.com
P.O. Box 5124
Gaithersburg, MD 20882
800-579-WIRE
custsrv@wigjig.com

**Sheila Hobson**
**Ebb Designs**
1162 Valley Road
Hockessin, DE 19707
302-239-0704
shobson900@aol.com

**Jeanne Holland**
**Vintaj Natural Brass Co.**
www.vintaj.com
P.O. Box 246
Galena, IL 61036
815-541-5558
Jeanne@vintaj.com

**Susan Karczewski**
**Purr-fectly Unique Jewelry**
1112 Brubaker St.
Warsaw, IN 46580
574-268-1110
purrjewelry@comcast.net

**Jan Ketza Harris**
**Jess Italia**
**Trish Italia**
**Galena Beads**
109 N. Main St.
Galena, IL 61036
815-777-4080

**Darien Kaiser**
7112 Pine Road
East Dubuque, IL 61025
815-747-8821
dkaiser@yousq.net

**Deanna R. Killackey**
1N526 Creekside Court
Lombard, IL 60148
630.336.9754
d_deluco@yahoo.com

**Janet L. Killackey**
3826 Saltmeadow Court S.
Jacksonville, FL 32224
904-992-7293
jkillack@comast.net

**Sue Kwong and Karen Li**
2310 S. Eighth Ave.
Arcadia, CA 91006
616-574-3186
heartbeads@adelphia.net

**Lynn Larkins**
**Lynnier Concepts**
228 S. First St., Suite 202
Milwaukee, WI 53204
414-765-0200
lynnierconcepts@fast-surf.com

**Dotsie S. Mack**
**Beadazzled, Inc.**
www.beadazzled.net
501 N. Charles St.
Baltimore, MD 21201
410-837-2323
dot.mack@mac.com

**Kathleen P. Manning**
**Beadazzled, Inc.**
1507 Connecticut Ave. NW
Washington, DC 20036
202-265-2323

**Barbara Markoe**
**Rituals Jewelry**
10668 Ranch Road
Culver City, CA 90230
310-202-7807
ritualsjewelry@ca.rr.com

**Deborah McClintock**
**Beadazzled, Inc.**
1507 Connecticut Ave. N.W.
Washington, DC 20036
202-265-2323

**Michelle McKenzie**
**McKenzie Glassworks**
www.mckenzieglassworks.com
20818 Tiger Tail Road
Grass Valley, Ca 95949
530-346-2068

*Wendy Mullane: Sienna Moon Medley.*

**Jenni Moore**
**Beadazzled, Inc.**
www.beadazzled.net
Tysons Corner Center 1
McLean, VA 22102
703-848-2323
mcbenno@gmail.com

**Mackenzie Mullane**
**Mac Mullane**
www.macmullane.com
P.O. Box 246
Galena, IL 61036
815-541-0219
mac@vintaj.com

**Wendy Mullane**
**Vintaj Natural Brass Co.**
www.vintaj.com
P.O. Box 246
Galena, IL 61036
815-541-0219
wendy@vintaj.com

**Christy Nicholas**
**Green Dragon**
www.greendragonartist.com
6434 NW 32nd St.
Gainesville, FL 32653
352-271-8477
greendragon@bellsouth.net

**Patrick Ober**
**Chainmail Armour and Jewelry**
Felton, PA
717-246-8674
armourer@earthlink.net

**Susan A. Ray**
**Bead A Simple Life**
www.beadasimplelife.com
Maquoketa, IA 52060
563-541-3307
raysa542@aol.com

**Cathie Roberts**
**Galena Beads**
109 N. Main St.
Galena, IL 61036
815-777-4080

**Barbara Svetlick**
**River of Glass Studio**
www.riverofglassstudio.com
1506 SW 24th St.
Fort Lauderdale, FL 33315
954-527-5528
bgumba@comcast.net

**Ronda Terry**
**Terry's Treasures**
www.rondaterry.com
586-943-5400
Ronda@rondaterry.com

**Cas Webber**
www.caswebber.com
CasWebber@mac.com

**Sandra Webster**
**Sandra Webster Jewelry**
www.sandrawebsterjewelry.com
5217 Old Spicewood Spg. Rd. No2003
Austin, TX 78731
800-934-9335
rwebster1@austin.rr.com

**Cindy Yost and Kat Allison**
**Guppy Sisters**
www.beadworkzstore.com
www.copperloom.com
111 Fischer Drive
Newport News, VA 23602
757-875-5156
copperleaf@cox.net

*Kat Allison and Cindy Yost:*
*Copper on Blue Bracelet.*

# More Beautiful Beading with Susan Ray and Friends

## EASY BEADED JEWELRY
75+ Stunning Designs
by Susan Ray and Sue Wilke

For beginners or advanced beaders, this book includes 75+ projects for creating gorgeous earrings, necklaces, bracelets, pins and more. Includes a helpful resource guide.

Softcover • 8¼ x 10⅞ • 144 pages
150 color photos, 100 illus.
**Item# EBJD • $21.99**

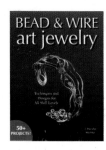

## BEAD & WIRE ART JEWELRY
Techniques & Designs for all Skill Levels
by J. Marsha Michler

Incorporates step-by-step instructions and more than 250 detailed color photos and illustrations to demonstrate wirework techniques including beading, hammering, wrapping and coiling, to create more than 50 exciting accessories.

Softcover • 8¼ x 10⅞ • 128 pages
250 color photos and illus.
**Item# EBWJ • $21.99**

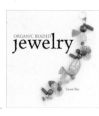

## ORGANIC BEADED JEWELRY
by Susan Ray

Learn how to expand your beading expertise by exploring new materials to bead. This book bridges the gap between the various materials used to create fine jewelry, and the techniques used to make unique pieces.

Softcover • 8 x 8 w/flaps • 160 pages
250+ color photos and illus.
**Item# ORGJW • $22.99**

## CREATING LAMPWORK BEADS FOR JEWELRY
by Karen J. Leonardo

Explore the world of lampwork beading through the 200 color photos and instructions in this unique guide, while you discover the ability to create lampwork beads and 16 related jewelry designs.

Softcover • 8¼ x 10⅞ • 144 pages
75 b&w illus. • 225 color photos and illus.
**Item# Z0975 • $24.99**

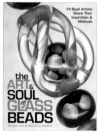

## THE ART & SOUL OF GLASS BEADS
17 Bead Artists Share Their Inspiration & Methods
by Susan Ray & Richard Pearce

Step-by-step instructions and beautiful photography show crafters how to create stunning necklaces, earrings, and much more with glass beads.

Softcover • 8¼ x 10⅞ • 144 pages
250 color photos
**Item# GLABD • $24.99**